# FABLES

*of*

# FORTUNE

WHAT RICH PEOPLE HAVE THAT YOU DON'T WANT

# RICHARD WATTS

# FABLES

### *of*

# FORTUNE

---

**WHAT RICH PEOPLE HAVE THAT YOU DON'T WANT**

---

# RICHARD WATTS

EMERALD
BOOK CO.

Published by Emerald Book Company
Austin, TX
www.emeraldbookcompany.com

Distributed by Emerald Book Company

For ordering information or special discounts for bulk purchases, please contact Emerald Book Company at PO Box 91869, Austin, TX 78709, 512.891.6100.

Design and composition by Greenleaf Book Group LLC and Alex Head
Cover design by Greenleaf Book Group LLC

Cataloging-in-Publication data
(Prepared by The Donohue Group, Inc.)

Watts, Richard (Richard Connell), 1955-
   Fables of fortune : what rich people have that you don't want / Richard Watts.
— 1st ed.

   p. ; cm.
ISBN: 978-1-937110-12-3
1. Rich people.  2. Wealth.  3. Rich people--Conduct of life.  I. Title.
HB831 .W28 2012
305.5/234                                    2011932964

Part of the Tree Neutral® program, which offsets the number of trees consumed in the production and printing of this book by taking proactive steps, such as planting trees in direct proportion to the number of trees used: www.treeneutral.com

TreeNeutral

Printed in the United States of America on acid-free paper

11 12 13 14 15 16   10 9 8 7 6 5 4 3 2 1

First Edition

*To my wife, Debbie, for encouraging me to share my thoughts.*
*My three boys, Aaron, Todd, and Russell, for honoring their parents.*
*My father, Tom Watts, for modeling a life of humility.*
*And to my grandmother, Pokie, for affirming my inner voice.*

*Special thanks to Sealy Yates and Brianna Engeler*
*for helping to materialize this project.*

# CONTENTS

# PULLING BACK *the* BROCADE CURTAIN

I am a keeper of secrets.

I am silence on the receiving end of a midnight phone call.

I am the facilitator of dreams.

I am a fixer of million-dollar mistakes.

I am a gatekeeper to keep the masses away.

I am paid to keep watch from the shadows.

Do you think you know what it's like to be rich? The yachts on the Mediterranean . . . the gold Rolexes and necklaces dripping with diamonds . . . the thirty-thousand-square-foot mansion complete with servants . . . the ability to play on private islands or at exclusive gaming tables in Las Vegas . . . the freedom from responsibility . . . is this what it means to be rich?

If you believe what you read, the life of the rich must be better than the life of the average Joe. In fact, their lives must be perfect, dappled with the gold of luck and good fortune. If only you could be rich, your troubles would be over, your worries melting away with an instant influx of greenbacks.

But when imagination gives way to reality, it becomes far too easy to look around with eyes of discontent. Why not me? I must not be good enough, smart enough, or lucky enough. Life dealt me a bum hand. If only . . . If only.

Unfortunately, most of us never know the real story. That's intentional. Behind the façade of fancy cars, glittering jewels, and designer clothes can be a hidden world of woe. Ruined relationships, shaky self-esteem, and overwhelming obligations head a list of uninvited sorrows that surround many of the super-wealthy.

My clients have experienced one or more of these difficult and heartbreaking lessons. I've been encouraged to invite you into the shadows in hopes that you may gain some measure of understanding that wealth has a cost. Let me open the curtains to let you see what the lives of the super-rich are really like. Let me show you a world beyond the tabloids and the "reality" shows. Let me reveal the secret reality behind your fantasy of being wealthy. Expect to find shadows of your own experience woven into one or more of the stories. Being rich may be more costly than you might imagine.

## IN THE INTEREST OF FULL DISCLOSURE

This book is not a professional or psychological study of the rich; it is a chance to look inside their world, to ponder questions you have always wanted to ask and find a few answers. I believe understanding the reality of wealth will provide an honest, comparative reflection on your own life.

The names of the characters in the book have been changed to protect their privacy, but they have asked me to tell their stories. Having successfully reached the summit after navigating many of the inherently complex problems of wealth, many individuals I have dealt with have managed to achieve fulfilled and balanced lives in spite of their wealth, not because of it.

They want you to know the truth. Once you see inside their daily difficulties, you might think of your place in life as a safe and welcoming refuge. You may discover your world, in some ways, is actually richer than theirs—in relationships, satisfaction, experiences, and fulfillment.

# PART ONE

## LIFESTYLES *of the* RICH *and* FAMOUS

# CHAPTER ONE

# THE HUNDRED-MILLION-DOLLAR DEFINITION

My occupation as general legal counsel to the super-rich gives me a window into a lifestyle most people never see and can't begin to imagine. In our celebrity-obsessed culture, the media focuses on a glittering façade of wild parties, gleaming luxury cars, and giant McMansions. But behind the scenes is another world that makes what we deem "wealth" seem like chump change. It is the world of the "super-rich."

Who qualifies as super-rich? Forbes magazine has suggested the classification of super-rich requires a net worth in excess of $30 million. The magazine defines net worth as a family's liquid financial assets—in other words, cash and investments, not including homes or other non-liquid assets.

In my clients' world having $30 million in liquid assets doesn't make you super-rich. That level of wealth requires putting a limit on spending. I define the super-rich as those who never have to ask themselves, "Can I afford this?" Their net worth is such that almost anything money can buy is within their reach at any time. They inhabit the economic stratosphere. In a sense, they spend their days shopping at the Mall of Life without ever looking at a price tag.

This stratosphere is rarified indeed, a financial altitude attained by either inheritance or remarkable luck; the V.I.P. lounge of planet Earth; the place where only the super-rich gain entry; an exclusive enclave most of us cannot begin to comprehend. For the great majority of us who deal in denominations of hundreds or thousands, the thought of hundreds of millions of dollars boggles the mind.

To join the fraternity of my clients, you would typically have a net worth of $100 million or more. I consider such people to be super-rich. To get an idea of how wealthy these individuals are, let's assume they earn three percent per year in passive income. That is $3 million in "mailbox money" coming in every year. My clients earn more in a year, without working, than someone making $50,000 per year will earn in sixty years. Only about twenty thousand individuals on Earth have this kind of net worth. That's a pretty select group.

Just to make it clear, let's look at a few examples to contrast the "rich" and the "super-rich."

Randy's company nets about $8 million per year from his international furniture-production business. His operation stretches from facilities in Vietnam and China to several in the United States. However, Randy has made very few investments outside the business, choosing instead to use most of the company's profits to further expand his enterprise. If his company fails, his sole source of income will dry up. When the remainder of his non-business assets is sold, the resulting cash and savings would not produce enough income to maintain his current lifestyle.

However, if he were to sell his company tomorrow and properly invest the proceeds, he would receive an average income of about $1.4 million per year. After taxes, he would have between $700,000 and $1 million of net spendable income. Most of us would wonder, "Who couldn't live on a million dollars a year?" But in Randy's case, he couldn't survive financially. His $18 million home and accompanying $12 million mortgage plus his four $250,000+ automobiles generate a burn rate of about $120,000 per month, not including household needs, travel, clothing, entertainment, and other expenses. In order to stay within his new budget, Randy would have to greatly reduce his spending, sell his home, and learn to live more modestly. By our new definition—quite different from the usual one—Randy is not truly wealthy. In a sense, the demarcation between those who are poor, rich, wealthy, and super-rich is somewhat relative. If Randy decided to take some of his chips off the table by deliberately corralling his extravagance and living in a home with no mortgage, he would be able to reduce his dependence on his company and maintain a fairly high level of wealth.

Unfortunately, no matter how much you have, you tend to want a little bit more. You crave the next level of everything, from golf courses to country clubs, from Mercedes to Bentleys, from ocean-view homes to beachfront homes. Most wealthy people seek to display a lifestyle of abundance, extravagance, and luxury that often borders on wasting money. Randy cannot—will not—let go of what he has now in exchange for long-term financial stability. He is wealthy but vulnerable; everything could disappear in a moment's time with a single stroke of bad luck.

Now let's consider some people who are truly super-rich.

On the island of St. Bart's, Gustavia is the place to see and be seen. Designer boutiques, high-end restaurants, and luxurious hotels come together to create a sought-after playground for the rich. The marina boasts sixty yacht slips and additional moorings in the harbor.

While my wife and I were on vacation, one afternoon we noticed a particularly striking yacht in slip number one. Painted in rich green and glossy white, it boasted twin spiral staircases reaching from the upper deck all the way to the dock. A matching helicopter stood at attention at the back of the boat; a large crew of handsome young men and one beautiful young woman, all dressed in impeccable whites, swarmed over the boat.

As we stood there, admiring the yacht, a crew member jumped down and joined us. "We've been here for four months," he volunteered.

"Really? Your boss must really like St. Bart's," I said.

"I wouldn't know," said the young man. "He hasn't arrived yet."

"What?!" We were speechless.

"Yep. He sent us here four months ago to wait in line for slip number one. We first dropped anchor way out in the harbor. Every night, as boats leave, everyone else is allowed to move up in line. We finally got to number one about a week ago. The boss won't be seen on the boat unless he's in the first slip, because it's the closest to the village and," he spoke under his breath, "the hardest to get. But today the crew was briefed he has decided to send the boat to Indonesia, so we're headed there tomorrow."

"Let me get this straight. Your boss sent you here months ago just to work your way up to this slip, and now you're heading to Indonesia instead?"

"I guess. The boss hasn't actually been on the boat in three years. He just sends us to places he thinks he might want to go. The family owns a home on the hillside in Gustavia also. The only one who has stayed in the home, to our knowledge, is his mother-in-law, who spends a week here each year. Last year she hosted a lunch aboard the boat for three of her friends."

I walked away, thinking hard. The slips started at $600 per day. That crew of ten or twelve worked full-time and traveled year-round. Maintaining a boat that large—not to mention the helicopter, its pilot, and its mechanic—had to be costing the "boss" at least $200,000 per month. And he hadn't used the boat in three years.

So why does he keep it? Because he can.

## BECOMING BULLETPROOF

Let's consider another example of the super-rich.

A friend invited me to tag along on a weekend hunting trip with a special group of hand-picked "superstars," individuals with phenomenal success stories. The jet-helicopter sitting on the tarmac when I arrived at the airport was my first clue this would be no ordinary jaunt through the woods with my trusty rifle, a sack of peanut butter sandwiches, and a case of warm beer. Leaving Portland, Oregon, at a speed of 130 miles per hour, we careened east up the Columbia River Gorge. I hung on tight to the seat of the $10 million helicopter, feeling like a contestant in a reality show that allowed me to be president of the United States for one day. Amazing. Exciting. Terrifying!

Forty minutes later, having crossed the entire state of Oregon, I saw the spectacular Highland Hill Ranch ahead, complete with private heliport and attendants anxiously waiting on the ground. When we touched down on the pad at the hunting lodge, I found myself in the company of billionaires, TV personalities, senators, and a celebrity or two. Our accommodations were lavish beyond imagination. We sat down to three-course lunches every day. My dirty clothes never hit the floor; they were whisked away to be washed and pressed immediately. The fields were stocked with prime targets, and as a group we brought in more than 750 birds over the course of our four-day stay.

You're probably wondering about the cost of our weekend getaway. I watched my host write a check for $90,000. Under my breath, I muttered, "My God, that's $120 a bird!"

Our host overheard the comment and chuckled, "The cost was actually $45,000, and the second $45,000 was a tip. Do you think they will remember me the next time I call for a reservation during high season? You want to bet they will squeeze me in somehow?"

My thoughts flashed to how generous I always feel when I

put an extra dollar in the tip jar at Starbucks. My host planned to return often enough—to re-experience what I considered to be a once-in-a-lifetime event—that he wanted to build a reputation with the staff. I just wanted the ego boost of hearing the employee at Starbucks say, "Good morning, Richard! The usual?" We live in different worlds.

I served with another super-rich individual on the board of trustees of a nonprofit organization. He had sold his grand-father's company for nearly a billion dollars. My friend owned several extravagant homes, three jets, and more than one hundred collectible automobiles in perfect condition. However, his standard daily attire consisted of an assortment of worn blue jeans, and he much preferred a meal of hot dogs and french fries over filet mignon and foie gras. He often asked his private chef to serve ballpark grub on one of his ready-to-fly jets. This man's disposable passive income from his assets was in excess of $90 million per year. That's "super-rich."

## AN ALL-ACCESS PASS

I've known Jen for years. She's an incredible success story—having worked her way up from an entry-level clerking job to become the chief operations officer of a major hotel corporation with several significant properties on the Las Vegas Strip. A few years ago, my wife and I hit Las Vegas for a long weekend of R&R. Jen was kind enough to put us up at one of her hotels, allowing us to stay in a magnificent suite.

We ate lunch together on Saturday afternoon, and as I was telling Jen how much we were enjoying all of the amenities in our room, she grinned. Then she said, "Where do you think the heavy hitters stay?"

"The penthouse? Right? With the best views, a butler, and maybe a piano? Maybe some great art?"

With a twinkle in her eye, she told my wife and me to follow her. We walked down to the casino floor and stopped in front of a simple door with a single security guard leaning against the wall. As a secret service agent in the White House might do, he nodded to Jen and opened the door to allow us inside.

I felt like I'd entered an alternate universe. A fifteen-foot-wide marble corridor stretched out in front of me; it seemed to go on forever. Every hundred feet or so, the ceilings soared to create a beautiful alcove, and arrangements of fresh flowers stretched at least six feet in all directions. The opulence was staggering. Renoirs rubbed elbows with Picassos and the odd Monet. Jen explained the floor had six rooms, and she opened the first door on the right.

We walked into a suite that had to be at least 5,000 square feet. Glancing around, I saw a stream of water flowing across the room and falling over a spill of river rocks into a crystal-clear pool. A cedar sauna, iridescent-glass hot tub, and heavy iron furniture added to the spa-like atmosphere. Turning around, I saw a 50-foot Bermuda grass putting green, then a music room with a grand piano, and finally a full-size kitchen complete with stainless-steel appliances and granite countertops.

"How much per night?" I asked.

"Oh no, this is all complimentary. These rooms would be at least $20,000 per night if we did rent them, but we don't. To stay here, you have to lose a minimum of $500,000 per visit. For those hitters, called 'whales,' the room is just the beginning. Gourmet dinners? Included. Expensive wine? Included. Fully stocked liquor cabinet? Included. Tickets to sold-out shows? Included. Masseuse? Tennis lessons? Personal shopper? Included. We even find out what thread count they prefer for the sheets on their beds before they get here. It's our job to make everyone here think they are the richest people in Vegas."

As we exited the suite and walked down the marble hallway, a man staggered through the door. Obviously very drunk, he was supported on both sides by two of the most gorgeous women I'd ever seen. My wife and I stopped in our tracks and stared as these six-foot glamazons propelled the slightly pudgy, middle-aged man down the hall and into one of the suites.

"Included."

Was this member of the super-rich truly happy? He was drunk, unable to appreciate his fabulous surroundings. Instead of enjoying the wealth of true love and affection, he was seeking some semblance of happiness in the arms of prostitutes. Was this super-rich individual any happier than we were? Not at all. Jen later explained the story behind this lucky gambler was a life of incredible sadness. He had been married three times. The children of the first two marriages were not speaking to him. The son from his third marriage worked in his company and rarely showed up for work. Like his father, he spent much of his time in Las Vegas showing off how much money he could afford to lose. His numbing agent of choice was nose candy, which was a downgrade from his prior addiction to meth. Yet everyone in the hotel was trained to jump at the command of either one of them. "Money," after all, is a respectable resume.

## HAVES AND HAVE NOTS

Money opens doors to a world most of us will never see. A four-month wait for a reservation at one of the country's top restaurants? Never. A single phone call guarantees a meal at the chef's table that very night. "Sold out" never really means "sold out." Front-row seats are instantly available for the right price. In material terms, the trappings of wealth are nearly limitless. If you can imagine it . . . and pay for it . . . it's probably within reach.

Late one evening, during the last leg of a personal vacation, my wife and I checked in at an expensive hotel in New York City. We were tired and wanted to get straight to bed. Unfortunately, we were mistakenly given the key to the penthouse.

In the center of these exquisite accommodations sat a giant, king-size bed made up with the finest of linens and surrounded by antique French furniture. On top of the entire bed and all over the floor steamed a two-foot-high mound of freshly popped popcorn!

The sight permanently twisted my conservative sense of romance. Nearly twenty-five years have passed since that night, but the smell of popcorn still evokes that memory. Like a couple of children walking into their parents' bedroom at the wrong time, my wife and I dove for the door and closed it behind us. We were speechless. All I could think to ask my wife as we returned to the lobby was, "I wonder if it was buttered."

Super-rich people are good-looking, well-dressed, physically fit, smart, exciting, and fulfilled . . . or are they? Our society tells us they are. Be honest: Isn't that what you think? According to Thomas Jefferson, every man and woman is entitled to "life, liberty, and the pursuit of happiness." While the great majority of us are still mired in the pursuit, we observe the rich and believe they have already won the race.

As we spy on the wealthy through the media or interact with the "haves" in our own lives, we receive a painful glimpse of our most private dreams and aspirations as they are lived out by others. In the marina, a tanned, glowing family may be laughing and smiling aboard the yacht you have dreamed about owning some day. On the garden tour you took last year, you sighed over the $10 million dream house you would have bought if you could. You would love to see the Eiffel Tower in Paris, but your ordinary life takes you on a business trip to Pittsburgh for your boss.

While you fold your knees into the six inches of space between your airplane seat and the one in front of you, the wealthy family boarding the aircraft ahead of you settles into spacious, first-class lounge chairs on their way to Europe for a vacation. Or, more frequently, their Gulfstream jet receives priority clearance for take-off ahead of your commercial jet, heading off for a private island in the Caribbean as you panic about making your connecting flight. They didn't have to strip down or be scanned by airport security. They have their own private terminal: "Have Nots Not Allowed."

Have your observations of the rich relegated you to a life of jealousy and envy? Do you feel "less than" because you lack the material trappings of the wealthy? When you daydream, are you caught up in what will be or what will never be? What would you give to join the ranks of the super-rich?

## REALITY CHECK

For most of my career, I have dealt with families whose net worth is in the $100+ million range. I've observed when most people attain enough extra money to fulfill their basic needs, they form a new wish list. Too often, as the money flow increases, so does the scope and length of this wish list. "Wants" become "needs." Before long, few recognize the difference.

Those of us without the problem of excess money dedicate at least part of our lives to dreaming about one thing, the one item we are sure we need to make our lives complete. Most of us firmly believe a boat, a luxury automobile, an exotic vacation, a second home, a larger diamond ring, a new wardrobe, a remodeled kitchen, a swimming pool, breast implants, a healthy retirement income, or $100,000 cash in the bank will bring fulfillment and happiness. In reality, we may never attain that one thing. But hope is a powerful motivator. While we work to attain our dream we must make do with what we have; as we do so, life force-feeds us a realistic perspective.

Although we may never be super-rich, we have moments . . . moments when we gain a little ground in the struggle, when we achieve a small victory, when the pressure lets up for just a second and we realize life is good. Everyone longs to be in that moment. But the super-rich, who live in that moment full-time, find it difficult to appreciate the privilege. They often miss the joy we find in everyday blessings: a healthy marriage, a close family, a position of respect in the community, a happy memory from childhood, or time with a few good friends.

"Whatever!" you say. "My life is pure hell, and I never feel fortunate to be who I am. My days are filled with endless scheduling hysteria, I barely get enough sleep to wake up and start again, and I never have enough money to meet my family's needs."

Granted, you may have only survived at times, but hold on to the truth that challenges and trials refine us. We become stronger and more resilient each time we come through a struggle on the other side. Simply because when we don't have more, we can hope for a better future—an improvement over what is and a dream for what could be.

After reading these stories, you might feel proud that the hard work and struggles of everyday life you face confer their own brand of personal satisfaction. It is not that the super-wealthy are unhappy all of the time. Nor is it my contention the poorest of the poor aren't miserable. The rest of us fall somewhere in between. And from each of our individual stations we look over the fences of our neighbors and compare lawns. We disregard our own blessings and overlook the others' negative attributes. Why? Because we think more is better. And more than anything, we desire more, believing it will make us feel better. It would. For a while.

I have spent the last three decades managing the affairs of super-rich families. Together, we make crucial decisions about how to handle difficult family issues, after which I am directed to execute their wishes. Quite simply, if you are not related by blood, you can't get to them without going through me. Lawyers, accountants, mortgage brokers, investment bankers, brokerage houses, real estate brokers, congressmen, senators, lobbyists, special-interest groups, contractors, property managers, landlords, corporate presidents, charities, salespeople of every variety, and occasionally the butler, chef, or gardener all want one thing: money. I am the last line of defense between the families I protect and the masses who want what they have.

My training at Harvard Business School and my law degree mean little to my clients. They can buy and sell a pedigree with pocket change. The privileged, the haves of the world, hire me because I speak two languages: the language of the super-rich and the language of the working American. From the perspective of the super-rich, their world is civilized and ours is uncharted wilderness. I am a scout. As Sacagawea guided Lewis and Clark into new, dangerous territory, I forge ahead to clear their way of unexpected complications, execute their directives, and minimize the contact with the outside world that often generates a significant amount of stress for them.

At the same time, I have spent my career dealing with problems created by wealth. As a man of faith, I know true wealth does not come from money, and people in the most modest circumstances can lead wonderful and fulfilling lives.

I also understand "normal"—our normal. Although today I am blessed with financial security, I remember what it is to be poor, to eat hot dogs and beans in order to survive until the next paycheck. I know what it's like to make Christmas gifts from supplies gleaned from clearance bins at a craft store because money is too tight to buy presents at the mall. I know what it is like to be married with a child and one on the way, working full-time during the day and going to class at night. I know this life, too. Those were good times. I just didn't recognize it at the time.

That is why you can trust me to be your guide as we enter the unfamiliar world of the super-rich. We'll experience shocking excesses and extreme sorrows along the way. It will be an exhilarating ride that will help you understand the meaning of true wealth. Shall we continue?

## CHAPTER TWO

# UNCOMMON LIVES

Dave and I were talking about his plans to propose to his girlfriend, Annie. "It has to be something totally unexpected, something no one could pull off . . . something our grandkids will tell people about someday. Wait. How about the Eiffel Tower on New Year's Eve?"

I need to mention this was November 1999. Welcoming the New Year and the new millennium from the Eiffel Tower would be impressive, to say the least. "Great idea, but there's no way to pull that off. Are you kidding?"

Six weeks later, on January 1, 2000, I got a phone call from Dave in Paris. "She said yes!"

"What?"

"She said yes! And you have to hear the story."

As my friend began to tell the tale, I felt my jaw sliding toward the floor. Apparently, he found out the Eiffel Tower restaurant was hosting a New Year's Eve dinner at $10,000 per couple. This was the most exclusive place in the world to have dinner at the turn of the millennium. Every table had been booked at least five years in advance. So Dave and Annie dressed to the nines and left their hotel in the early evening. Dave had hidden $10,000 cash and an engagement ring in his pocket. His mission was to gain entry and conquer the Eiffel Tower.

When they reached the elevator, the security guard stopped them. "Sir, the Tower is closed for a private party tonight. I must see your passport to confirm you are on the attendance list."

"I don't think I am on the list, but I'll give you $500 to let me take my girlfriend up on the elevator and just walk around before the party starts."

The guard pocketed the money, and up they went. Once they reached the restaurant level, Dave and his girlfriend stepped out to enjoy the view. He slipped away to speak to the doorman at the restaurant. "Are there any reservations available for tonight?"

The doorman could hardly contain his laugh.

"Well, can I take my girlfriend in to see the restaurant?" Dave asked. With a $1,000 handshake, they were inside.

As Annie walked around the restaurant, watching the staff set up for the night's bash, Dave found the maître d' issuing orders near the kitchen. "Do you have any tables left for this evening?" Dave grimaced.

The man stopped, held up a dismissive hand, and asked Dave how he'd managed to get inside. Grinning, Dave spread his hands and revealed a roll of $100 bills (about $5,000 worth). The man's eyebrows shot up. Dave mildly asked, "Couldn't you just shove a little table over there on the side? We'll sit anywhere. And we won't eat much."

The maître d' grabbed the cash and pulled over a busboy. Within seconds, Dave and his soon-to-be-fiancée were sitting at a table against the window, looking out over all of Paris, ready to attend the most exclusive New Year's Eve party in the entire world.

They partied with royalty from all over Europe, shocking and entertaining everyone they met with the unashamed story of how they had crashed their way into the party. They dined on lobster, Russian caviar, foie gras, and other delicacies prepared by Michelin-starred chefs. They sipped the finest wines and toasted the new millennium with Dom Perignon.

At the stroke of midnight, Dave asked Annie to marry him, handing her a five-carat, custom-designed Neil Lane ring.

After she said yes, Dave paid the bandleader $1,000 to play some current dance tunes rather than the orchestral stuff they had been playing. Then he grabbed the microphone and told all of his new friends Annie had agreed to marry him. The crowd cheered, and Dave dared them to join him on the dance floor. But there was no dance floor. Easy fix for Dave. Another $1,000 and tables were being moved to accommodate the crowd's request.

The party continued until 4:30 in the morning. They danced until they couldn't dance any more. Then, with the last of his cash, Dave paid the kitchen crew to make breakfast for everyone. When the revelers began to stumble out the door, they each wanted Dave's card and contact information. He made dozens of new friends and contacts that night. In fact, he has visited many of them over the past few years. They couldn't get enough of the creative, fun-loving party crasher.

Neither could Annie. They were married six months later. I guarantee their children and grandchildren will be telling that story again and again.

Riches do afford uncommon access to remarkable experiences. The rich need only think of an adventure and they can make it happen. What fun! There is no denying it. But unlike my friend Dave's experience, these opportunities are most often about things and places . . . not people.

## THE QUALITY OF THE ORDINARY

When we think of a winter vacation, most of us imagine driving to the closest mountain range and checking into a modest hotel with our family. We spend the days hauling equipment up the mountain on creaky lifts and winging our way down the slopes with the frosty wind in our faces and a sense of great exhilaration. We spend the evenings ordering pizza and watching a movie, resting up for the next day of fun in the snow. After a few days, it's time to drive home, telling stories about our most spectacular thrills and spills all the way.

In contrast, the super-rich board their private jets for Aspen or the Swiss Alps, and their drivers ferry them to their own spectacular vacation homes. Others check into the Four Seasons or Ritz-Carlton for a week or two. Their skis are checked by the valet, waxed, tuned, stored, retrieved, and carried to the slopes each day. When they want lunch, snowmobiles are available to whisk them to a lodge that features a five-star meal and a famous "has-been" ski legend mingling with everyone as if he cared they were there. Then they spend their afternoons with a dashing ski instructor from Turin, Italy, who promises to make them ready for the next Olympics, so long as the tip is good.

On their way to another gourmet meal, where the only sounds are the clinking of silver against fine china plates, perhaps the rich might pass the local pub, where the meek and mild hang out after an exhausting day of skiing. Happy hour means plenty of cheap beer and bar snacks. The room is crowded and noisy; the regulars openly mingle with strangers. In one corner, a group is howling with laughter over the story of one man's close encounter with a tree stump and an errant ski pole. Another is celebrating the completion of his first black-diamond run. The off-key strains of "Happy Birthday" float in the air.

Most of the super-rich would never contemplate stepping into a bar for a $2 beer and a few minutes' camaraderie with a bunch of sweaty strangers. But in many ways, they may be missing out. Genuine friendship grows out of shared successes and failures. Isn't it comforting to laugh when life's wrestling match gives you an hour or two to rest before throwing you to the mat again? Those of modest means appreciate a reprieve from the workaday world and modest accomplishment. Our perception determines our perspective.

## SOMETIMES MORE IS JUST MORE

Never assume the person doing something more expensive than you can afford must be having a better time than you. Sometimes more is just more.

Often the wealthy have so many opportunities for pleasure they become easily bored with even the most remarkable experiences. Imagine learning the art of fly-fishing. The super-rich hire an instructor who schools them quickly in the skill of casting. A professional guide takes them to a stream in Montana or Patagonia, Chile, to a spot where the fishing is epic. The guide selects the proper fly for the water's speed and clarity, the size of the fish, the time of year . . . and surprise! They immediately catch the limit their first time out! Challenge met. Fly-fishing is checked off the list. Another outing would be redundant.

Compare that to the child who is taught fly-fishing by his father. Years of effort go into learning each nuance and skill. More years are spent finding the good fishing spots. Some are winners; others yield nothing. When is it best to go? What conditions favor good fishing? What bait is used in different conditions? How do you tie a dry fly as opposed to a wet fly? If we were to ask that fly-fisherman, "What do you know about fly fishing?" he would tell hundreds of stories about his adventures with his dad. His passion for the sport is probably contagious. Try to compare that lifelong passion to the most expensive guided fishing expedition money can buy.

Years ago I decided to take each of my three sons on a once-in-a-lifetime trip when they reached the age of thirteen.

Motivated by a desire to invest in memories to be revisited with my progeny for decades, we carefully planned every detail of our itinerary. I went all-out to give them the best experiences I could afford.

My firstborn, Aaron, and I traveled to Alaska to hunt bear. Leaving Los Angeles behind, we flew to Anchorage, then caught a prop plane to a lodge near the Tsiu River Delta. We camped on a glacier with Scott, our guide, for three days of the two-week trip.

Portions of our trip required rigorous climbing and belaying down rocky cliffs. The night sky was filled with sparkling stars, and we could hear giant Alaskan brown bears sniffing at the entry flaps to our tent. We experienced elation and exhaustion, sweating and shivering, utter tranquility and abject fear. Each moment burned an indelible mark in our relationship.

Together, Aaron and I stalked and bagged a black bear. After taking Aaron's trophy, we walked down the Tsiu River with fishing rods. We hadn't planned to fish, but the steelhead salmon were running, and we couldn't pass up the opportunity. In two hours we caught sixty-three fish between us. It was too easy, so we threw down our rods and started skipping stones on the river. Every fisherman I know has listened to Aaron's story of steelhead fishing in Alaska like he was describing a personal encounter with God. At the time, the ease of our catch made the experience seem common when it was anything but.

My other two boys, Todd and Russell, traveled with me separately to Zimbabwe and New Zealand. We had incredible times together. You would think these experiences should have defined my relationship with my kids, eclipsing anything else we did together. However, extravagance does not always result in excellence.

At the time, these trips depleted most of my savings. The planning was well intentioned. But the resulting memory was an inferior return on my investment. Simply said, the trip was my weak attempt to equal what the super-rich might do with their kids. And my kids didn't get it! If you ask my boys about their favorite childhood experiences, long before they mention my "trips of a lifetime" they'll tell you about the YMCA Indian Guides.

Indian Guides is a children's program sponsored by the YMCA that provides opportunities for fathers and sons to spend time together. When my boys were young, the program cost $45 a year per child (with a $10 discount per extra child). Initially, I didn't want to participate. My wife signed me up anyway. Wives have a wonderful way of knowing what our children really need.

The program consisted of "tribes" of dads and sons (between the ages of five and ten) who met at a different child's home every two weeks for fun and fellowship, including a story, a craft, and a snack. Each year, we attended three weekend campouts together at regional campgrounds. All of the tribes in the Indian Nation came together for the event; we were part of the Naswawkee Indian Nation group, along with three hundred other pairs of fathers and sons. The dads organized the tribal activities and barbecues, and purchased all the food and snacks. A nighttime ceremony involved an exciting story told around the campfire.

We were an impressive group of inexperienced campers. Doctors, lawyers, mechanics, construction workers, plumbers, bartenders, teachers, electricians, asphalt layers, pool cleaners, real estate brokers, and stay-at-home dads were represented. Pitching our tents provided a source of great amusement the first night as every dad struggled with the task while his seven-year-old son read the tent-assembly instructions aloud.

All told, my sons and I struggled and laughed together through thirteen years of Indian Guides. We went on thirty-nine weekend campouts, which cost a total of $10 each for the park entry fee. Dirt, hot dogs on a grill, and campfire stories added up to the most fun we ever had.

## THE TRUE VALUE OF PERSPECTIVE

International airports are crisscrossed by high-speed human conveyor belts that shuttle passengers to baggage claims and airline gates. Some people stand to the right while on these "flat escalators," taking a moment to rest their weary arms and legs via the wonder of modern convenience. Others rush by on the left, carelessly slinging their carry-on luggage into anyone who might be in their way. The speed of the conveyor belt isn't enough; they want to move even faster, get there a little more quickly, save time that probably will be spent later waiting at another gate or for a taxi.

A few choose to walk through the concourses under their own power. Perhaps a little exercise is in order, so these individuals take the opportunity to stretch their legs before or after a long flight. Very rarely, a traveler will stroll down the corridor, taking his or her time. All of these people are heading to the same planes and baggage claims. What they may have failed to consider is they'll all depart or collect their luggage at the same time, regardless of the method they choose to get there.

Why do most of us believe quicker is always better, sooner is preferable to later, faster is twice as good as slower, and richer bests poorer? Does our destination change if we reach it a few minutes sooner? Is a reward more meaningful if it comes now rather than later? Who proved that faster is something to be proud of? Does the mere fact of having wealth make life more significant?

Our perception usually determines our perspective. When traveling on the human conveyor belts, the only times we physically feel a difference are the moments when we step on or off. Within seconds, speed becomes relative. The only way to tell we're moving faster than normal is by looking at the people who aren't on the belt. To the passenger who opts to walk next to the flat escalator, you appear to be effortlessly passing them. But if we look down at our luggage and keep our eyes on the path itself, we seem to be moving at a normal pace.

Albert Einstein believed if we were able to travel at the speed of light, time would stand still. In theory, we could board a train that moves at a rate of 186,000 miles per second and arrive at our destination at the same moment we left. On the train, time would seem to pass normally. Only when we stepped off the train would we realize time had not advanced. Time would be relative to our situation.

In the same way, wealth is relative. Most of us stand on the concourse of life, watching the rich pass by at a faster pace. We envy the conveniences they enjoy and assume our lives are common and boring in comparison. We imagine the wealthy spend endless hours each day swinging from one passion to the next, experiencing an endless itinerary of life's "Disneyland" attractions, one more exciting than the last. But be realistic. How many roller coasters do you think a person can handle in one day without becoming bored or getting motion sickness? The super-rich may travel on the speed walk, but from their perspective they are moving at a normal pace.

Some of the super-rich fear anything that might be perceived as ordinary. They value the perception that they are different, that they are the haves of the world. The rich often pride themselves on uncommon lives and constant new experiences. Whether or not they offer true satisfaction and fulfillment is a perspective that is difficult for the beholder to evaluate.

When the haves seek to entertain themselves, they look outside. When the have nots look for entertainment, they look inside.

In other words, when the super-rich get restless, their money gives them access to a lot of things—trips, boats, cars, houses, entertainment from outside themselves. When one experience becomes common or ordinary to them, they become complacent. So they find something else to acquire or do. On the other hand, when regular folks get bored, they have to look inside to what they already have for activities they enjoy doing, rather than relying on other things to entertain them.

If you are super-rich, perhaps you might recognize a lesson from the financially modest. Their weddings may not have a thirty-piece band, but their DJ will have you dancing your shoes off instead of just being a spectator in the audience. It takes a strong will to accept humble surroundings, to cope with the perils of every day, and to find fun in ordinary things.

# CHAPTER THREE

# GIVING *a* LOT *for a* LITTLE MORE

I typically avoid French restaurants, not because of the food, but because of the quantity and price of the food. The appetizer typically fits on a teaspoon, the salad requires a specific tiny fork, and when the main course arrives I see more plate than food. The bill always comes on a very small receipt, and the bottom line is typically large. I appreciate value in return for my hard-earned money, and meals like these feel abnormally costly. I'd much rather have a char-grilled hamburger and a dish of homemade ice cream in my own backyard. Six bucks never tasted so good.

But French restaurateurs are actually wise. They sell the experience of dining. They know a select few will pay a lot of extra money to feel a sense of elevated service, to be greeted by a haughty maître d' in a tuxedo and spoiled by table-side preparation. The owners of such restaurants recognize their patrons want to be treated like kings and queens, and they create a sense of exclusivity and foster the perception of quality through the presentation of fine furnishings, crystal, china, a snooty waiter, and a big-name chef.

Why the small portions? The French are also experts in teasing the appetite. They know their food is rich and filling, so they balance a diner's desire for exclusivity with an unfulfilled appetite. Portions are just shy of the additional bite that would completely satisfy your hunger. You leave wanting more.

## DEFINING VALUE

The super-rich are ready and willing to pay whatever is required to receive better service, treatment, and quality. They want to achieve an experience few have ever realized. They determine value by exclusivity.

I remember an anniversary dinner at my wife's request at Le Cuisine, an expensive French restaurant in Orange County, California. The people at the table next to us ordered coffee and eight individual shots of Napoleon brandy that cost $250 an ounce. Two waiters arrived at their table, one with a cart carrying freshly brewed coffee and the other with a handheld platter of crystal shot glasses already filled with the precious liquid. To our horror, the host at the table instructed the second waiter to pour each shot of brandy into a cup of coffee. Without showing any hesitation or emotion, the waiter replied, "Of course, sir," and poured $2,000 of brandy into $40 worth of coffee. As I witnessed the event, I realized each shot glass of brandy cost more than my entire anniversary dinner.

I can't imagine ordering Napoleon brandy—its exclusivity doesn't add enough value for me. If I had tasted it, I would not have known or cared about the difference between expensive brandy and regular brandy. Plus, my wife would have immediately recognized and pointed out she could have bought multiple new dresses for the same price as something she doesn't even like. Celebration over.

## DIMINISHING RETURNS

The newly rich perceive value because everything they ever wanted to purchase or own now seems cheap and easy. When money becomes no object, every purchase is a "deal." At first, every acquisition offers a sense of value because it was previously unattainable but no longer represents a significant expense. But over time, the sense of value diminishes with each purchase. They feed at the table of materialism without ever being satisfied.

When Peter was first referred to me as a client in 1996, he arrived with what he perceived to be a huge problem. He worked as an interstate truck driver for a large moving company. Every Friday he returned to his one-bedroom apartment in Westminster, California. On the weekends, Peter worked as a handyman for several local homeowners.

An elderly woman named Annette lived in a ramshackle house on the Seal Beach waterfront. She was elderly and lonely. Peter had his hands full with service calls from Annette because her home was quite old. Peter was Annette's only real contact with the world. She always made him sandwiches and invited him in for visits. For five years he fixed her faucets, mowed her lawn, rewired electrical malfunctions, and spent time talking with her about unimportant and trivial things.

On a Monday morning, Peter sat in my office nervously awaiting a legal consultation. He had never been in a lawyer's office. And even though he had done his best to clean up for our appointment, his fingernails were permanently stained with dirt and his shirt needed a good washing.

"Annette is dead," he muttered. I remember thinking, Criminal law is not my area of practice, and it sounds as if Peter needs a defense attorney. Then I thought about the pocketknife I kept in the top drawer of my desk and pondered whether I could inflict much damage if this killer tried to assault me. Peter passed a torn piece of an Albertson's brown grocery bag across the top of my desk. With two hands, he gingerly turned and centered the brown paper on my desk so the writing was facing me.

Nearly illegible handwriting was scrawled across the front in gray pencil. Each letter was an inch tall or more: "I, Annette Simpson, give all of my property to Peter Corin, dated May 5, 1996." She signed the letter in an even larger hand.

That was all. Annette had died of natural causes.

Peter inquired, "What does this mean?" He didn't seem to want the answer.

"Well, it depends on who Annette Simpson was and what property she had when she died," I counseled. He hadn't given me much information. "This is called a holographic will, and as long as it is dated and in the handwriting of the testator, it is as legal and effective as any will or trust."

Peter squirmed in his chair. "I was afraid you might say that. She owned an old house with a few sticks of furniture." He fidgeted with his car keys. "I'm just a simple guy with simple needs. I have never had anything worth much. I wouldn't know what to do with that house." His next question took me by surprise: "Do I have to take it?"

"No," I said. "You can just rip up this paper, and her property will go to either her heirs—if she has any—or the state of California."

"She didn't have any children," he reluctantly volunteered.

Peter didn't mention Annette's home was situated on one of the most expensive stretches of coastline in Southern California. After my staff completed a title search, we learned Annette not only owned the home and lot; she also owned three other oceanfront lots next door. Peter never thought about the "lots next door," where Annette had asked him to mow down the weeds three times a year.

Peter became a multimillionaire in an instant. Oddly, his new fortune seemed to make him extremely uncomfortable. A more accurate word might be horrified. He started calling me every day with concerns about the properties. Peter told me he would gladly sell all of the property to me for $200,000. This was one of the greatest tests of integrity I have faced during my legal career; a multimillionaire was willing to sell me his estate for $200,000. Instead, I offered to find a listing agent who would assist him in selling the house and lots. Ultimately, Peter received a seven-figure down payment in cash and a promissory note secured by each of the four properties that would yield him a monthly income of tens of thousands of dollars for decades to come.

My job as his legal counsel was complete. Peter's present financial situation and future security was like Fort Knox. But his life was about to unravel. First, without asking anyone, Peter bought a Kenworth diesel big rig. He had never bought anything new before, but he had always wanted to pull his own cargo. Peter became an independent interstate trucker. He appreciated the realized value from his purchase; the truck met his expectations perfectly. Peter thought the salesman was sincere when he said the $125,000 list price on the tractor was the lowest the dealer could accept to sell the vehicle. Peter also assumed because he paid cash, he didn't need to insure the truck.

His brother-in-law Bill suddenly took a great interest in helping Peter with his money. Within a week of disbursing the funds, Peter and Bill came into my office. Bill had convinced Peter to invest $500,000 in his accountancy practice. Bill signed a promissory note—unsecured by any collateral—that entitled him to make interest-only payments for ten years at an absurdly low interest rate. My hands were tied; Bill was a previous client, and giving advice to either party would have constituted a conflict of interest. I did share my opinion that it is never a good idea for family members to invest with one another. Bill took Peter to another lawyer, and the deal was done. Six months later, Bill convinced Peter to accept $50,000 as payment in full for the remaining balance owed on the note. Peter lost $450,000 to his opportunistic brother-in-law.

Next, Peter decided to upgrade his living standards. He could easily afford it. So he purchased a home on the beach and purchased not one, but two new cars to fill the garage. He paid retail for everything. Peter hated confrontation; he didn't want to ask for a deal.

Simultaneously, he began to purchase things he didn't really need. One day, Peter remembered his father had taken him hunting when he was a child. With great nostalgia for "the good old days," Peter started collecting expensive rifles. He planned to learn how to hunt again. But somewhere around the purchase of the fifth or sixth rifle, he lost interest. In the months that followed, he gave his rifles away. They didn't hold any value.

As he continued to maneuver for more and greater material gain and personal excitement, he forgot about the activities he used to enjoy—tinkering, fixing things, and taking hikes on the local mountain trails. The menu of acquiring more things was on the table, and he was busy letting the main course of materialism dictate his every move.

Twelve months later, Peter appeared in my office once again. He had bailed two nephews out of jail, given several supposed "friends" money to start businesses, and bought a new Harley Davidson motorcycle that had been promptly stolen because he left it out on the street at night. He had crashed his uninsured Kenworth while hauling cargo, damaging another vehicle and injuring the driver. He was being sued and was paying for the cost of an attorney because he had no insurance. His life had become hell.

In a panic, Peter sold the mortgages he held on the three oceanfront lots to an outside investor for fifty-five cents on the dollar. After paying the legal fees required to get Peter out of trouble, he declared bankruptcy. Peter left my office on the verge of a nervous breakdown, unable to enjoy a moment of his life.

Sadly, I never saw Peter again. Bill, his brother-in-law, died of cancer six months later at the age of fifty-five. The strain of the $500,000 loan debacle had broken their relationship. Peter did not attend the funeral. The family was no longer on speaking terms. According to his sister Mary, Peter returned to the alcoholism of his distant past and left the state permanently.

## THE DISEASE OF MATERIALISM

I wish Peter's story was an exception, a single cautionary tale gleaned from years of interaction with the rich. Sadly, I see "Peters" all the time. Any sense of value tends to fade away when money is no object.

The progress of this disease may not be as rapid or evident as it was in Peter's case, but most of the wealthy experience an elongated version of the same situation. The postscripts are often similar. The super-rich crave the passion that materialism has depleted. But without a sense of value, satisfaction remains elusive.

You can characterize money as being similar to alcohol or drugs. When it is used intermittently and in relatively conservative portions or doses, the results can be enhancing and beneficial. But as in any substance abuse, as the use becomes continual and excessive, it becomes more and more difficult to regain a personal base line. That is, it is hard to recognize the difference between "a little" and "a little more." Before long "a lot" becomes normal, and the notion of going without becomes unacceptable, unachievable, and often terrifying.

Many people set a limit for drinking: three beers or two glasses of wine per day—that's it! Yet, because there is no warning label on money, people of wealth continue to buy one thing after another, adding to their possessions and increasing their comfort level without regard to the effect of the constant purchasing on the peace of mind and character of the individual and the family. Materialism is very subtle and contagious. As with any disease, hosts can be affected in different ways and to varying degrees. A husband saddened with the pressures of maintenance of wealth can suddenly be on a different playing field than his own wife. The wife may accelerate her spending, activities, and interests, and before long they may hardly recognize one another. Children can be even more difficult to harness. Left unmanaged, children, even adult children, typically drink the Kool-Aid a lot faster and with less regard or even recognition of the consequences. In short, to be successful at running the gauntlet of materialism, the skill set of discipline and self-denial must be at such a self-actualized level that such a person would hardly have use for the money.

On Crystal Cove Beach in Newport Beach, California, the autumn sun is setting. A circle of friends from an inland city are huddled around a campfire with beach towels wrapped around their damp swimsuits. As they share stories and laughter, the last hour of a good day passes slowly. The ribs they barbecued earlier were burned to a crisp, but the watermelon was ice cold and dripped down their chins. Each person enjoyed every precious moment to the fullest and received a sense of value in return.

High above the beach, a single resident sits in front of a 60-inch plasma-screen television, alone in her $25-million mansion. Her window is open, and she can hear the laughter of the group below. They glance up and notice the woman as she walks out on a balcony and stands motionless, looking out over the few remaining people on the beach. "She owns the beach," they think. "We only get to do this once a year, and she sees this paradise every day. If I only had her life."

But they don't understand. She no longer sees the beach. One of life's great vistas has lost its value for her. Envying someone else's "everyday paradise" can blind you to the value of what you yourself have achieved. She would give much to be able to appreciate a little mindless laughter, a group of good friends, and a plate of burnt ribs.

# PART TWO

## SOAP-OPERA FAMILY DRAMA

# CHAPTER FOUR

# THE MONEY-PROOF MARRIAGE

A striking young woman visited my law office for a consultation. She was dark and beguiling, with piercing blue eyes and shining dark hair. Her short, black dress paired well with black stilettos and red lipstick. Completing the vision was a small valise with an understated Prada logo.

Victoria introduced herself, held my outreached hand a little too long, and then confidently entered the conference room. She sat in the chair closest to me and elegantly crossed her long legs. She didn't waste any time. Opening her briefcase, Victoria slid a thick 1040 tax return in my direction and asked, "How much child support can I get?"

The tax return was that of a very successful man about forty-five years of age—twenty years older than Victoria. A wealthy doctor, he had built an impressive list of real-estate holdings through wise investments. His annual income at the time hovered near $700,000. This man was also the son of a significantly wealthy family in the area.

In those days, Orange County calculated child support in a straightforward manner. Basically, an attorney would enter the incomes of each spouse into a court-approved computer program, and it spit out the average child-support ruling in a dollar amount. "In my opinion," I responded, "the guideline indicates child support of between $10,000 and $12,000 a month until the child reaches eighteen years of age."

Victoria changed the subject, "Do you charge for portions of an hour for office consultations or do you have a minimum of one hour?" I had hardly finished my one-sentence answer that the first consultation was free of charge when she stood, packed her papers, shook my hand, and swiftly left the office.

Exactly one year later, Victoria reappeared in my conference room. A six-week-old infant boy in a car carrier rested on the floor of the reception area. When my assistant inquired about the baby, Victoria dismissively waved her hand and said the baby would be fine by himself.

"I want to retain you," she stated. Her demeanor was calm and contained. In a matter-of-fact tone, she challenged me, "But if you are going to be my attorney, you will have to be ruthless." She smiled, which struck me as odd and disquieting, considering, as I assumed, she was about to divorce her husband.

As it turned out, she wasn't requesting a divorce at all. You can't divorce a boyfriend. I soon discovered when she had first appeared in my office, she wasn't even pregnant. Her boyfriend was her boss. She had taken a job as his secretary, and after obtaining his tax returns she decided to make a small investment of her own. Her brief affair with the clueless doctor would land Victoria thousands of dollars in child support for eighteen years.

Her goals were quite clear. She demanded his vacation house at the beach, a brand-new Range Rover, and $15,000 a month in child support.

Months later, I heard Victoria had received every single one of her demands. Unsurprisingly, the doctor's wife was not amused by the tryst and its repercussions. In an acrimonious divorce settlement, she demanded and received the amount of Victoria's payoff many times over.

Doc is now living in a small apartment, working around the clock to support three children from his once-idyllic eighteen-year marriage and the love child of a one-night stand. He shouldn't have . . . But he did . . . Now he's done.

## WEALTH AS A WEDGE

What is it about wealth that often causes marriages to fall apart? What goes wrong? What changes? Who falls out of love? Who cheats? Who gives up? Who becomes unhappy first?

The average divorce rate in our society hovers at fifty-one percent over a lifetime; more than half of people who divorce remarry at least once. The divorce rate soars among the rich to almost seventy percent, with the majority of marriage casualties happening in the second and third generations of wealth. Multiple marriages are quickly becoming the norm. And in my experience, the high rate of divorce among the super-rich does not reflect the high numbers of spouses who might as well be divorced. They remain in their marriages for the sake of convenience and preserving financial stability. Love isn't part of the equation any longer.

Perhaps to better visualize what goes wrong in a marriage of the super-rich, or the haves, we should look at the more typical marriage. What goes right in a healthy marriage without wealth? What does an "ideal" day look like in a healthy family? Mom and dad go to work each day. They are both involved in caring for the children, including helping with the schooling, shopping, clothing, feeding, nurturing, teaching, and assigning and monitoring chores. Additionally, each parent has to share the upkeep on the home, weekday and weekend children's activities, providing transportation, keeping the children's schedules, and serving as ever-present psychologists.

Typical married couples must manage their time very carefully. Much of it is spent providing for others, so there is usually little time left for enjoying life. They have to deliberately schedule activities for family fun. In a perfect world, this kind of family regularly travels to a lakeside or riverside campground to bond with each other. This family piles into the car and drives to visit extended family members for holidays. This is the family that books a third-class trip aboard the Disney Cruise Lines and talks about their adventures for years. They will probably never venture far from home—no exotic trips to desolate islands with private homes, no villas on Lake Como in Italy. But they value every moment they have together.

Too often the members of this "average" family think life

is passing them by with no time for anything but working, eating, sleeping, and working again. However, from the outside it is clear this is a busy and happy family on most occasions. Of course, they struggle with the usual hard knocks of life. But because of these difficult times, family members have to interact with one another on a daily basis. In a functional family, good relationships are enhanced, and bad relationships result in confrontation and subsequent mediation. The most valuable keys to the survival and growth of such a marriage and family are the times they spend together and their dependence on one another.

What happens when we add wealth into the mix? Wealth can enable people to have more free time and opportunities. But subtle differences begin to creep in as a couple begins to accumulate wealth. Money becomes an end in itself rather than the means to an end. This couple begins to divert more and more time and thought to increasing wealth, preserving wealth, and utilizing wealth.

Developing a successful business is a difficult task, and it provides both monetary reward and a sense of personal satisfaction. The spouse who is primarily responsible for the growth of the wealth usually allows it to enter and climb up high on the family's priority list. Spouse, children, friends, and other priorities move down to accommodate the business. As the business grows and wealth increases, ancillary opportunities arise, such as golf or fishing, business trips, and social events with business acquaintances only one spouse knows well. Because of office politics and common interests based around the business, social events may be forced or uncomfortable for the spouse who is not involved in the business. At such events, or even when the other spouse appears at the office, a sense of awkwardness can become apparent. Or employees may pay special attention to the boss's husband or wife without building any real relationships. At home, conversation is often business centered.

Cracks appear in the marriage. Family members fail to spend time with one another and to pay attention to each others' needs in favor of the acquisition of wealth. When spouses spend more time immersing themselves in the trappings of wealth rather than in each other, they "grow apart." Relationships become stagnant, underappreciated, and ultimately strained.

In truth, wealth should not be a priority; it is best seen as a facilitator. Money should enable us to concentrate on the true priorities. Properly utilized, wealth can allow you to maintain your essential priorities—especially your family—and to add others to the list, such as friends, charity and volunteer work, philanthropy, and more.

As families move from rich to wealthy to super-rich, the issue of control begins to rear its ugly head. A business can and should be tightly controlled. Employees either do what they are directed to do or they are terminated. Everyone treats the boss more or less like a king or queen. Not so with a spouse. He or she does not see or treat the person in the same way. What began as an equal partnership will dissolve if one spouse tries to exert control over the other. Firing a spouse requires a very expensive lawyer and about half the value of everything you own.

Also, acquiring wealth of the magnitude I am talking about usually takes most of a lifetime. Often such divorces come after thirty or forty years and a fistful of children. They are very complicated and extremely painful for everyone involved.

## SHIFTING SANDS

Wealth is a subtle mistress. It smoothes out the rough spots in life, opens doors to previously unattainable opportunities, and provides you with comforts . . . yet all the while it is undermining your relationships.

Allow me to use a crude metaphor for a moment. Wealth can be like snorting cocaine. It seems fun and exciting at first; the rush is addictive. But eventually you can't recognize when you are high; you become aware of the drug only when you don't have it. Each time, you need a little more to feel the same ecstasy.

Al Pacino's character, Tony Montana, in the movie Scarface starts out dirt poor. His initial desire is to obtain respect from others, so he begins dealing drugs. As he terrorizes everyone around him, he becomes more and more successful. But then he begins to want the same lifestyle as the wealthy drug dealers in his circle. He buys the fancy home, the expensive cars, the beautiful girlfriend, and the entourage. In the end, the movie strikes a metaphorical high note when Tony begins to use cocaine because nothing ever satisfies his inner hunger. The cocaine that has made him rich becomes his executioner. In one final binge, he pours a pile of cocaine on his desk and buries his whole head in it in order to fill his nostrils and lungs with the drug. He has found no value in all of his acquisitions, and life has lost its meaning.

The super-rich become addicted to the possession of more and more. With each material gain they are disappointed because they perceive less and less value.

As people acquire wealth, they can become addicted to the "rush" of acquisition and luxury. Plus, many become surrounded by a crowd of people who are always pursuing more, bigger, and better—carrying them along in the sprint toward the same. New friends suggest extravagant trips, outings, and events, and spouses are often swept along without choosing to be, or they are left behind.

Unfortunately, each time spouses let go of the support and memories they have built together, they lose familiarity with themselves. Longtime spouses have traveled through life together; they know each other intimately and accept each other in spite of their flaws. New friends or associates only know people by what they appear to be. This shifting sand of identity quickly buries integrity and character.

As spouses let go of the old and put on the new, it is only a matter of time before the oven of life bakes a new set of personalities. Many of these couples begin to fight, perhaps because the spouse is the only person left who still knows who the other one used to be. Each begins a new life apart from the other, and before long they don't recognize each other.

## MAINTAINING A MARRIAGE

How do some typical marriages avoid these pitfalls?

At the end of the day, many people go home to their spouses and families. They may not be perfect, but they are generally there. They show up! They share their love through the hard times when life is ugly and painful. They also rejoice when life is good. Together, couples make do with what they have.

Our spouses can be a source of perpetual energy, turmoil, and joy. When you wake up at night and see your spouse sleeping next to you, what do you see? Has she stood by you for a long time? Has he done his best to provide you with a worthwhile life? Has he or she worried about the welfare, care, and health of your kids? Has he or she made you feel like you deserve to be alive and loved?

If so, you are truly wealthy in the ways that really matter. Don't be too concerned about the people with the $500 down pillows. They may look across the bed and see someone they don't recognize.

# CHAPTER FIVE

# CHILDREN *of* ENTITLEMENT

Most parents dream their children will have better lives than they did. In recent generations, "a better life" has become defined by financial stability. What a narrow definition! What about the development of strong character, integrity, a good work ethic, and healthy relationships?

It's ironic that the rich hope to help their children avoid the same toil that gave them so much satisfaction. When Michelangelo was asked how he had envisioned his masterpiece David within a giant hunk of marble, he responded, "David was inside the rock all along. My only job was to remove the unnecessary rock from around him so he could escape." Too many rich parents fear the pain that will come when they remove the rock around their children, so they never allow them to escape and become "works of art" as adults.

Make no mistake; the development of "children of entitlement" is almost exclusively the fault of the parents. In the name of protecting their children, parents create a disconnect between the "safe" or "ideal" world in which their children live and the real world. Wheat cannot grow without winnowing away the chaff, corn cannot be harvested until the stalk is cut, and a healthy adult will not mature without exposure to difficulty and pain.

Wealthy parents usually don't notice how easy it is for their children to have everything they desire and do whatever they want. Children don't have a built-in warning light. They have no foundation from which to understand that such behavior will cause them to take their privileges for granted. Any sense of appreciation or gratitude falls by the wayside in favor of the belief that they are entitled to or are supposed to have everything they want. Because no earning takes place between acquisitions, purchasing a new car or house feels equivalent to obtaining a new bicycle. Value never enters the equation. Consequently, there is a "richness" missing from the lives of these children. Perhaps the only way to savor the richness of life is to experience being poor.

One afternoon, I visited a couple at their home. When I arrived, they told me their fifteen-year-old son, Brian, was in trouble. I quietly continued to listen as they expressed their disappointment, and then I sat back to observe.

When Brian arrived home after school, his dad and mom were waiting for him on the front porch. To the average teenager, that would have signaled some sort of trouble. But Brian was oblivious to any wrongdoing. He nodded at them and started to go inside.

Dad stopped him in his tracks. Brian had borrowed his father's credit card, searched the Internet, and bought a new

Bose stereo system complete with extra speakers. When the boxes arrived, his parents immediately thought someone had stolen their credit card, but they soon realized something else had happened. Usually, if you steal a credit card, you steal the stuff you buy, too. Upon investigation, they found out it was Brian who had ordered the $3,000 stereo.

When they confronted their son, he comfortably admitted without hesitation he had made the purchase. "Why?" they asked.

He answered, "I ordered this for my birthday because it's coming up in two weeks. You were going to buy me something anyway. I just ordered what I wanted to save you the trouble."

The two parents looked at each other with an "Uh-oh, we forgot about his birthday" look, and they drilled down again. "Why did you use Dad's credit card?"

His rapid answer: "Because you can't write a check for an Internet purchase, and I avoided paying sales tax by purchasing the stereo out of state."

Again, his parents looked at each other as if the explanation had shed a whole new light on Brian's decision to make this transaction. They lost focus on the amount of money he had spent, his need for the gift, or the fact they might have liked to contribute to its selection.

There was a strange lull in the conversation. I realized Brian had explained his actions well enough to satisfy his parents. I struggled to keep my opinion to myself.

In a matter-of-fact tone, Brian then told his parents he had discovered Bose had recently marketed a new and better model that cost only $1,000 more, and he had already ordered it on the same credit card. Mom and Dad made a feeble attempt at scolding Brian for spending the extra money without their permission, but he was already leaving the patio headed for video games in his room and other pressing distractions on his day's agenda.

Brian turned back at the front door and yelled back toward the patio, "Dad, the old stereo needs to be repacked and returned. Could you take it to the office and have one of the shipping workers return it?"

Dad grumbled at his wife as if he disapproved of this inconvenience, but he didn't say a word to Brian. The matter was closed.

Children of humble families who invade the economic space of their own family interfere with the family's ability to manage their everyday financial needs. If a kid from an average family charged unexpected items on a credit card, mom and dad couldn't make their mortgage payment. Most children wouldn't imagine doing something like that to their parents. The level of financial accountability is high, and punishment for ignoring it is immediate.

But for the super-rich, no amount of expenditure on the part of the children will interfere with the family's functioning or lifestyle. Spending is not tied to economic survival, so children can acquire material things relatively unnoticed. Wealthy parents must be vigilant in order to notice the infraction.

Parents of "children of entitlement" often feel betrayed

and underappreciated. Their children independently develop a spoiled attitude that makes them undeserving of a parent's respect, "especially after all we have given them." Many parents respond by first withholding parental approval and then stanching the flow of money. The end result is a breakdown in the parent-child relationship.

## THE CONSEQUENCES OF ENTITLEMENT

Imagine taking a lion cub out of the wild, teaching it to suck on a bottle, and raising it in a beautiful enclosure. If we were to remove the bottle and put a live rabbit in the cage, the lion cub wouldn't know what to do with the rabbit. The lion only knows the bottle. Therefore, it would only understand it was being denied sustenance. Given enough time to develop a raging hunger, the cub will eventually bite the hand that feeds it rather than the rabbit.

Bill Oscar was forty-eight years old, the oldest son in a super-rich family. The senior Oscar, who started with nothing in Nebraska, had taken his ambition and a little seed money to the West Coast in the 1950s. Several decades later, the family owned more than a thousand apartment units in Los Angeles and nearly twenty-thousand acres of farmland in the Los Angeles Valley.

Bill was in charge of overseeing the property side of the business. Hired managers were responsible for each building, but Bill was in charge of collecting the rent and paying the expenses monthly.

One morning, Bill sat at my desk with guilt written all over his face. He confided in me that the scheduled rents totaled nearly $200,000 per month, but only $180,000 ever made it to the bank. He listed vacancies on the books even though the units weren't vacant. Then Bill confessed he was appropriating $20,000 a month for his own needs. He explained he was living with a girl who had insisted he give her an American Express card so she could maintain the type of lifestyle she wanted to live. Bill had bragged to her about the wealth he had gained from his own investments. His girlfriend was calling his bluff. She charged more than $10,000 every month. Bill thought he would lose her if he cut off her allowance, but I think his motive had more to do with his ego.

When I suggested his actions amounted to a criminal offense—probably a repeated felony—Bill laughed incredulously. "This is my money," he said.

"Actually," I explained, "it is your mother and father's money."

Bill declared that using money from one's own family could not be a crime. "Aren't I legally entitled to it?"

Somehow he had rationalized that because of my role as his parents' attorney, telling me would clear his conscience. Because I was the family counsel, he assumed I would not tell his parents. This forty-eight-year-old married man with children was a thief, taking from his family to support the shopping habits of his mistress. But he felt entitled to help himself to whatever he wanted.

When Bill's parents found out, they acted mildly disappointed, chose not to confront him, and hired an independent property manager to collect the rents in the future. Basically, Bill's parents treated the situation as if he did not have the proper skill set to handle his job. Following the same pattern, they did not mention the incident to his brothers and sisters. Why risk family disharmony? The matter was closed.

Sometimes you just have to recognize and admit the animal on the leash is calling the shots. By the way, the girlfriend bolted three weeks later, on to greener pastures.

## COMPRESSION AND EXPANSION

Most of us experience a life filled with repeated fluctuations of compression and expansion. Difficult times last for a while, and then when they let up for a moment, we can move forward. Compression can be caused by both internal and external influences. Internally we struggle with our own egos, our ambitions, our sense of personal worth, our societal position, our self-image, our images of how others perceive us, our health goals, our addictions, our failings, and our feelings of being financially successful and good providers, to name a few. Externally we get a promotion at work, we get a raise, the economy is healthy, interest rates are low, our neighbors are gracious to us, or we get fired, lose our home to foreclosure, lose a parent, wife, or child, get a traffic ticket, or find our automobile just decided to quit running. Others have characterized this journey as traveling through the hills and valleys of life.

If you believe you can avoid these rhythms at any income level, you are being unrealistic. They find everyone. Many people believe money relieves these symptoms of everyday existence. One thing is undeniable: There is a direct correlation between people feeling better as compression ends and expansion begins. The burden is temporarily lifted, and for a while life lets out a big sigh of relief and the mind experiences a moment of contentment.

Oddly, most parents could be convicted of trying to make our children's lives easier and less taxing than our own. Such parental ethics are either well-intentioned errors or just plain laziness. There is nothing better for children than to crash and burn as a result of their own errors in judgment and mistakes, for them to experience the consequences of their choices. You can tell a child not to put her hand on a hot stove ten times without success. It only takes letting her insist on it once for the child to learn the lesson.

There are occasions when the super-rich put their kids on a course for destruction at the advice of professionals.

One of the wealthiest families in our country sought the advice of the best estate-planning lawyers. Such lawyers are schooled in methods of maximizing the intergenerational transfer of wealth with the minimum amount of tax. They do not have training in the psychology of what happens to the children afterward, like a cruise-missile guidance engineer whose only concern is successfully delivering the payload to its target. They are not aware of or responsible for the explosion and collateral damage at the destination.

For this super-wealthy family, estate-planning attorneys created an irrevocable trust that delivered $50 million of the family's estate to their two heirs with less than half the typical gift or estate tax. Success! Not really. What the parents didn't realize was the trust was not revocable. The parents could not change the terms. The children were in their twenties, and the trust was set to trigger distribution twenty years later. Why be concerned now? But the twenty years sped by quickly, and when the children were in their forties the money was distributed. By then, with twenty years' growth, the principal had grown to more than $100 million. With no oversight or training, the two children took on their newly acquired wealth in the best way they knew how.

To address the insecurity each child felt living life as the child of a local mogul, they addressed their deficit with excess: limousines, jets, mansions, lavish parties, numerous relationships outside their marriages, drugs, and alcohol. The dad, still a conservative billionaire and a gentleman, lives with the disappointment of children who are an embarrassment to their community. This family's story is truly an example of converting a liquid asset into a long-term liability.

My own family has difficulty with these issues. No one is immune. And as the numbers get larger, so does the proportional damage to our kids.

Several years ago, my son called me in a panic. Actually, it was more of a confession. Over four years of college, unknown to me, he had racked up nearly $45,000 in credit-card debt. He had been juggling seven different cards companies had offered to him while he was in college. His mother and I paid for his tuition, and he was supposed to be on a fixed monthly budget. Apparently he felt the need to keep up with the partying and travel habits of his classmates, many of whom were given credit cards when they started college for discretionary expenses. The interest alone on his credit cards was more than $700 per month, based on an average interest rate of twenty-one percent, and his required monthly payment was nearly $2,000. It would take him twenty years to pay off all the debt.

His mother immediately ran to his defense, citing his good grades, his tenacity in securing a job two weeks after graduation, and his past record of little or no delinquency. My wife and I did not see eye to eye on my decision, but however painful it was for her, she honored my wishes. I gave my son two options: (1) Declare bankruptcy and live with the credit damage, or (2) Follow my rules for handling the debt. He chose the latter. Here was the deal:

- I would consolidate the debt to a six percent loan on my house.
- He would pay $700 per month until it was paid, and *all his extra income, raises, and bonuses would go to the debt.*
- Finally, he had to promise to own no credit card of any kind.

These sets of conditions became known in my family as FBC (Financial Boot Camp). Because this monthly payment was one-third of my son's total income, he was forced to give up his apartment and move in with three guys, sleep on a couch, and share a bathroom with two other guys for two years. He made sack lunches to take to work and bummed rides home to save gas. He learned to take dates to happy hours where he could buy a $2 beer and get free food. It was humiliating for him to say "no" to invitations from coworkers to go out to dinner or away for the weekend. He stayed home.

His mother and I could not discuss the arrangement, as she still felt my solution was cruel and punishing. It was terrible for me, too. On the first of each month, I would go online and check the loan to make sure the $700 had been paid on time. Each month the principal was reduced about $500. A twenty-three-year-old's lifestyle was severely diminished because of a monthly payment. But it was his payment. And the cause of that payment was his choice also.

After two years, he applied and was accepted to business school.

"What about the payment, Dad?" he asked.

I replied, "The payment is still due. You have to figure it out."

He was able to secure a partial student loan to make the payment for twenty-four months of business school. He became a bargain animal in business school; he refused to own a car, rented or bought used furniture for next to nothing, and then sold it for a modest profit at graduation.

We still had one final hurdle. The balance due was $23,000. Through his own persistence he secured a job as an investment banker at J.P. Morgan in New York City. His signing bonus netted him $25,000. That day he called, "Dad, I have $25,000 in the bank for the first time in my life and a massive student loan. You said four years ago I had to apply any bonuses I received toward the debt until paid. The day has come."

I pushed the phone aside as I sat at my home computer that morning to mute the lump in my throat that was causing me to choke.

"Jump on your computer, Dad, and pull up the credit card account. Tell me the balance."

"$23,142," I said.

There was silence. He had set his account for an electronic payment transfer.

"Watch the balance, Dad!"

Before my eyes the balance I had monitored every month for four years changed in an instant to $0.00. Lesson over! What he said next I will never forget.

"Dad, it sure feels good to be broke!"

What he never knew was how his father sat at his home computer that morning and wept with pride. But it's not about the parents, it's about the children. Children need to be in charge of their destiny. My son has developed a wealth of integrity in the process. His mother now says the whole plan was our idea as parents.

Most of the super-rich never experience compression. Generations grow up in a state of continual expansion, never going through the learning process that comes when we deal with problems or times of want. As a result, most of them are ill-equipped to handle even the smallest of life's obstacles.

In the economic slowdown that began in 2008, many of my "bulletproof" clients became very concerned about their financial status. One multimillionaire presented a spreadsheet that broke down exactly how much his wife was spending on Starbucks per year—around $3,400. He asked her to make coffee at home until the "squeeze" eased. Another man with a net worth of more than $200 million began to drive on side streets rather than paying tolls on the highway. Those who have been brought up in an atmosphere of constant expansion react strongly to the threat of compression—whether or not they will actually be affected by it in a meaningful way.

The super-rich often deny their children the opportunity to develop integrity through experiencing compression. They deny their kids the satisfaction of earning things on their own and the fulfillment that comes from a job well done. Sadly, what begins as an act of love often ends in the decimation of a child's character.

## COLD CASH AND COLDER HEARTS

Children of wealth and their financial advisers often use the phrase "liquidity event." This seemingly innocuous term holds a dark meaning; they are talking about mom and dad beginning "the big sleep" and the money finally showering down.

I've spent countless afternoons sitting in conference rooms

with super-rich parents as they listen to their children plan and scheme about how to bring mom and dad's ship of wealth into port with the least amount of taxes paid. Their entire motivation is to retain the greatest amount of money for themselves.

Lawyers, accountants, and advisers join in the process of "estate planning," in which mom and dad are persuaded to either relinquish ownership of their money in the form of various trusts and tax shelters or to just give money to the children. One creative fifty-three-year-old "child" coined the phrases "warm money" and "cold money" to define, respectively, money that is received as a gift during the lifetime of the parent and money that is transferred after the death of the parent.

Children of entitlement tend to take an inappropriate interest in the mental acuity of their parents as they age. In a normal family, when mom and dad become a little bit eccentric as time goes on, the children tend to leave them alone to enjoy their senior years without too much criticism. They chuckle when mom gives the grandchildren the same Christmas presents as last year or dad loses his keys . . . again.

But when children of entitlement see any decline of mental clarity in their parents (real or imagined), they often become very "concerned" about the well-being of their parents and the empire their parents are managing. Many times the children will hold meetings without mom and dad present to discuss their concerns. The ultimate result is usually an attempt to wrest control of the cash away from mom and dad.

These children of entitlement don't recognize the nature of their offense. They don't comprehend the disrespect inherent in their actions. Mom and dad brought them into the kingdom of the wealthy a long time ago, and preservation of the family wealth is the kids' highest priority, at least until they have control of it. Mom and dad—the ones who generated the wealth—may conveniently lose control over their own finances.

Have nots tend to see parents as parents rather than as a luxury cruise ship complete with captain and crew. When you go over to your mom and dad's house for dinner, you take your spouse and kids, a salad, a board game, and a few family stories you probably repeat too often. As a parent, when you tell your favorite joke for the millionth time, your children won't exchange looks and begin to plan a secret family meeting in order to discuss your mental health. They'll probably laugh right along with you. Your grandkids will sit in your lap without putting their hands in your pockets.

Your legacy will be shaped by what you actually do rather than what you have. With no kingdom to run, you will have more time, which is the real treasure in this life. Your descendants will remember you as "father" or "mother" rather than "founder."

Consider the advantages of raising children in a world where needs and wants are clearly defined, where money is something to be earned and handled with care. Your children will respect the way you provided for them. When they become parents, they will begin to understand the sacrifices you made and respect you for them.

# CHAPTER SIX

# THE DANGERS *of* INHERITED WEALTH

The Petrov family is Czech. Or maybe it is more accurate to say they *were* Czech, because every part of their family heritage, customs, traditions, and values is gone.

Mom and Dad Petrov grew up in poor households. Their parents emigrated from Czechoslovakia in the 1920s along with many others who wanted to pursue political and spiritual freedom in the United States. Grandma and Grandpa Petrov did not seek riches; they sought opportunity. There is a big difference.

Opportunity is a state of mind. It satisfies at every level of human desire. As long as we have opportunity, we have hope. And when we have hope, we become motivated to achieve our goals through hard work and persistence. Ultimately, this kind of opportunity is not about wealth, but contentment. It is about getting to a place where our basic needs are met—food, shelter, transportation, utility bills, education, and so on. Opportunity is a cycle of setting and reaching goals.

When we no longer need to work hard to meet our needs,

the opportunity for achievement is diminished. We fail to set and renew goals; things come too easily; we often lose our focus. Satisfaction and contentment are ideas to be chased. The very act of reaching them can cause the beginning of personal stagnation.

## MAKING THE MOST OF OPPORTUNITY

Papa Petrov decided to move his family near Palm Springs, California. Pursuing the goals instilled in him by his parents, he worked in the industrial sector for most of his life. His wife was the consummate mother. They had three beautiful boys in about three years.

Then, when Papa Petrov reached his sixties, he was forced to retire from a life of strenuous labor in the factory. Because he was frugal to a fault, he and Mama Petrov had saved a tidy sum of money along the way. He recognized his adopted hometown was situated along a path of growth in the Inland Empire, a dry, windswept valley between Palm Springs and Los Angeles. Papa Petrov began purchasing small commercial sites with a variety of tenants, including convenience stores, markets, post offices, and strip malls. Over the next twenty years, he accumulated mobile home parks, shopping centers, apartment buildings, mini-storage units, and some valuable raw land. The value of his properties skyrocketed. His income soared, and he became one of the wealthier landowners in Riverside County, California.

But Papa Petrov never owned a new car . . . and I mean never. He could easily have built a mansion, but he, his wife, and their three boys lived in a plain three-bedroom home on a busy street. The accumulation of riches wasn't on his list of goals and things to accomplish. He was more concerned with value and opportunity, with the journey rather than the destination.

## THE DRUG OF INHERITANCE

Papa Petrov pushed his boys to find their own way . . . or at least he tried. But they unavoidably lived in the shadow of his success. The boys asked for cars, but they didn't get them. They lived according to their parents' standards; they wanted more, and they knew it was available.

The Petrov children began to disguise their wants, claiming to seek their own opportunities for personal advancement. Papa Petrov invested capital in each son's business or aspiration, but he required them to work hard at their chosen vocation. Any request for additional capital prompted a lecture about work ethic and a barrage of criticism. Before long, his sons kept quiet, pretending to be content with the lifestyle they could afford.

Papa Petrov lived to be seventy-six and died of a heart attack. Mama Petrov lived another fifteen years. She wasn't as adept at holding the reins on her team of sons as Papa Petrov had been, and they stampeded her with constant ideas for the use of her wealth. Slowly, she succumbed to the boys' incessant requests to begin distributing some of the family treasure.

At first, their reasons included legitimate concerns like sending her grandchildren to college. The sons' arguments were persuasive: "Times were different when you were raising a family, Mom. Today everything is more expensive; college tuition has skyrocketed, and kids today want more." They made it sound like her grandchildren wouldn't survive without the influx of at least part of the family wealth. Mama Petrov's resolve weakened with each request.

When she transferred ownership of the first of the large apartment properties to her boys, each one began to receive approximately $50,000 per year. One by one, the Petrov sons quit working full-time. The eldest son pursued money as a vocation. Mama Petrov called me periodically, usually in distress or tears. She could not understand why the boys were becoming so aggressive about their financial needs. Next, she allowed the distribution of some of the smaller apartment buildings and commercial properties. The sons teamed up to purchase life insurance for Mama Petrov at a cost of more than $60,000 a year, ensuring they would receive another $3 million upon her death; their reasoning was they would need help paying her estate taxes. Who paid the premiums? Mama Petrov, of course.

## THE CONSEQUENCES OF WEALTH ADDICTION

Our conversations over the ten years that followed will remain in my mind forever as a forbidding commentary on the pitfalls of inherited wealth. The eldest son started to hobnob with the wealthy people in nearby Beverly Hills, continually returning to his mother with promises of surefire investments. He pushed and pushed for the use of family funds for investments; he was certain he could maximize Mama's income and increase the estate.

Since her daughters-in-law didn't need to work together with their husbands, conflicts arose, and soon each of the boys was divorced—the oldest son three times. The grandchildren became entrenched in bitter jealousies, dividing the family over trivial issues. One father and son stopped speaking; their rift continues to this day.

I fought to secure enough money in banknotes to provide for Mama Petrov. If financial decisions had been left to the eldest son and his children, they would have removed the family wealth completely from her hands. She wouldn't allow that. Neither would I. I had made a promise to Papa Petrov.

Like a narcotic that's taken too often, the pursuit of riches is an addiction. After a while, most people who experience wealth become dependent on it. Eventually they don't care where it comes from or what it takes to get more. They just want a continuous flow, preferably in increasing amounts. Watching Mama Petrov as she was pursued by her children and grandchildren in the last years of her life was incredibly heart-wrenching.

When I attended her funeral, I spoke of one of the most kind, loving, modest, and gracious women I had ever known. The boys appeared to be united in their grief, but arguments over the management and distribution of the properties were already raging. Each brother teamed up with another on one issue and heatedly opposed him about something else. The strong undercurrents of bitterness and jealousy flowed freely.

In the parking lot of the church, after the service and before the procession to the cemetery, one of the Petrov children approached me. He obviously had rehearsed his speech, "Mama thought of you like a son. I know you loved her. Can we meet at your office tomorrow with my brothers to discuss distributing the rest of the money?"

My response was curt. "Let's hold this discussion until your mom is in the ground." He didn't notice the sarcasm. In fact, he nodded as if he concurred with my suggestion. "Good idea," he muttered, as he returned his hand to his mother's casket as it was being wheeled to the waiting hearse.

## INTEGRITY AND INHERITED WEALTH

A local shop owner who is aware of my profession and my specialty in managing wealthy families once asked, "Is the old adage about the third generation losing all the money true?"

Good question.

In order to understand the truth behind this statement, we have to address the differences between the children of the haves and the children of have nots. First, children of the haves are typically rich from birth. As they grow up, the presence of money is a fact of life, and the trappings of wealth are everywhere. Second, the opportunities and experiences afforded by the presence of wealth—with a few exceptions to prove the rule—lead to an attitude of entitlement. The sons and daughters of a rich family struggle to comprehend the privilege of having money. They didn't earn it, but they are accustomed to it. They unknowingly become dependent on riches, expecting to have just about every-thing they want, everything they don't know they want, and, most important, many things they really don't need.

The first generation to obtain wealth is usually a hard-working couple focused on a family enterprise or business. The mother and father start with little or nothing. They typically concentrate on providing basic necessities. Every decision is infused with a sense of deep concern about surviving slumps in the economy and other factors that might affect their income and threaten their ability to provide the bare sustenance of food and shelter. At some time in their careers they have to go with-out; they become "penny pinchers." They understand value. An automobile that costs $10,000 and provides transportation is sufficient for their needs. Mom and dad would never consider buying an automobile that costs $12,000 because it looks better or is more popular. They funnel the $2,000 they save into other parts of the family budget. In simple terms, they make sacrifices to attain their top priorities of providing for the family in the present and planning for the future.

As time goes by, mom and dad "make it." Their company begins to generate excessive amounts of money. Do they choose to drive Bentleys? Not usually. Mom still looks at the meat counter and considers the cost of top sirloin versus filet mignon. She may buy the filet, but she does so with an appre-ciation for the difference, for the ability to purchase the more expensive meat. She will never forget the sacrifices she and dad made to be able to purchase the filet. Mom and dad never take their good fortune for granted.

Now let's consider the children, the second generation. Are they innately spoiled? I've always been interested in that word. According to Webster's dictionary, spoiled is defined as "to strip of natural covering, to impair the quality or effect of something, or even to rob by force."

Some of the children of wealthy families exemplify this definition. They have been stripped of their natural covering, and their ability to appreciate their blessings is usually impaired. The question becomes "Who is robbing them of these things?" At first glance, only two parties are involved: mom and dad, on the one hand, and the children, on the other.

But perhaps another factor is at work. Wealth is like a giant reservoir. As mom and dad continue to fill it through their hard work, it eventually exceeds the needs, wants, and desires of the family and begins to overflow its capacity. Imagine Lake Mohave in Nevada. Mom and dad may have once been laborers whose sole desire was to fill the reservoir, bucket by bucket, in order to provide security in case of a drought. Those days are over. They are operating Hoover Dam. After the water leaves the dam, the flowing river carves its way through natural terrain. The water may cut one way in a certain type of rock and in a different way in another. But make no mistake; either the flow will result in downstream irrigation and abundant crops, or it will create the Grand Canyon.

Once a flood of wealth is released, each child will be affected in a different way. The natural character of each child is often stripped away by the unrelenting flow of water. A few may channel the flow positively, utilizing the wealth for the benefit of the family, company, and community. But the majority will be swept away by the promise of unbounded materialism.

No matter where a child is downstream, it is always easier to live along the banks of a river than it is to walk into the hills and create your own reservoir. The second generation has difficulty understanding sacrifice, the decision to give up something to obtain something better later.

Unfortunately, children of wealth understand little about their supply of water other than the fact that they live on a river and it always keeps flowing. In law school, my professors taught that people who own land along a river have "riparian rights," the right to consume the water flowing across their property, no matter its source. They are entitled—with some restrictions—to consume it or at least a portion of it. The second generation of wealth often exhibits the obliviousness of entitlement. They expect to have everything, and they assume they deserve it.

The third generation—the grandchildren—hardly have a chance. They never heard the stories of how mom and dad made it because they inherited it; they never learned to respect the sacrifices that made their current lifestyle possible. Children of entitlement give birth to a generation with no sense of the value of wealth. Though they may have the best intentions and want to give their children every advantage, the second generation didn't earn the money, rarely sacrificed, and don't model the behavior of discretion and discernment that a child needs to learn. Typically, the dam breaks in the third generation, the water flows without restriction, and the valley below the dam is flooded.

## PRICELESS POVERTY

In essence, being "poor" is having nothing and knowing it. Being "rich" is having everything and knowing it. Being "entitled" is having everything and not knowing it.

Our three sons grew up in a middle-class home. Sometimes we had and did nice things, but most of the time we lived a relatively normal lifestyle. When my oldest was admitted to law school, he declared he wanted to obtain loans and pay for his education on his own. "This is the only way I can own my career," he insisted. We let him. He flourished. His brothers hated him for the precedent. My fondest memory is of the time he called me at the end of his first year, excitedly telling me he planned to treat fourteen friends to home-cooked New York strip steaks for dinner at his apartment. Immediately, his mother and I were concerned about the frivolity of his action . . . until he explained he had sold his first-year used law school books for $86 and bought the steaks at Costco with the proceeds. Now that's the way to leverage one's assets.

My youngest son, Russell, just graduated from college and is living on his own, working full-time in order to save for his future goals. After his own round of Financial Boot Camp (FBC), Russell pays all of his own expenses, including gas, insurance, credit cards, and even Starbucks. He packs a lunch to take to work every day and, at least for now, barely covers his expenses. His mother and I could make this easier . . . but don't.

I am also very thankful when I consider Papa Petrov. He worked most of his life to get ahead, and in doing so he unintentionally made several generations of Petrovs unhappy, caused divorces, fostered broken relationships between siblings, and left his wife to die frustrated and unappreciated. His grandchildren are currently immersed in the process of losing every dime.

How about your family? Do you have meals together? Do the grandkids come over on weekends to play at Grandma and Grandpa's house? Do you vacation together? Do you first think of the love you have for each other before you consider your parents as the providers of your dreams or sources of endless financial support? If you can answer any of these questions in the affirmative, then count your blessings. You are not mired in the trap of entitlement, and you cannot enable children of advantage.

Perhaps the only way to savor the richness of family life is to experience some form of poverty.

The next time you sit with your adult children, thank them. Thank them for allowing you to grow old with dignity and without assault. Thank them for praising you for your real achievements and holding you accountable for your shortcomings. Thank them for accepting and continuing the family traditions you hold as important because they understand why they are important. But most of all, thank them for permitting you to unconditionally love them and discipline them, for allowing you to celebrate their strengths and their accomplishments, and for looking to you in times of weakness or setbacks. They will thank you for allowing them to experience life on their own terms.

# CHAPTER SEVEN

# UNDER *the* THUMB *of* RICH IN-LAWS

The Campbells were worth more than $100 million in 1969. Dad Campbell's story was a compelling one, a rags-to-riches saga of a common farmer turned land baron. He built and controlled a manufacturing empire. I remember walking through one of his warehouses; its four walls stretched around an entire city block.

A friend of mine began dating Angela, one of the two Campbell daughters. Bill married Angela in a royal extravaganza. My wife and I had never experienced a spectacle quite like it, and their marriage seemed to have an auspicious beginning.

## TRADING AWAY IDENTITY

Within the first few months, Dad helped the young couple to finance the purchase of a brand-new home in an upscale private community. Because Bill was educated as a high-school teacher, his salary couldn't pay the property taxes on their home, much less the mortgage. So Bill took a position in the family business, managing the customer service department. Dad Campbell arranged to pay him three times as much as the position would pay a non-family member.

Angela had never been denied anything by her dad or mom. When she wanted a new car, she simply asked for one. Without any discussion with her new husband, Angela drove up in a new car. She wore expensive designer clothing and carried a company credit card. No one asked her to turn it in when she got married. She loved to shop without ever looking at a price tag. Monthly statements were paid by the company comptroller. The word budget didn't apply before her marriage, and Angela and Bill never discussed one after the wedding.

From the outside, you might think Bill had won the lottery when he married Angela. But in my years of experience in dealing with the super-rich, I've discovered, as a rule, the day a non-family member takes the first dollar or job from the family, he or she immediately loses a level of respect in the eyes of the in-laws. Why? The patriarch of a wealthy family typically achieves his position by a focused and unrelenting commitment to hard work. The fact that a non-family member gets access to wealth by marriage (for "free") is like a speck of sand in an oyster that begins to cause irritation from day one. But the end product is never a pearl; it's a festering ulcer.

The newlyweds started hot out of the blocks, and within a year they seemed to be far ahead of the rest of their peers. They bought a real estate lot on the beach, then designed and built a new home three times larger than any of our modest homes. They bought fancy cars, had a new baby on the way, spent weekends at the family lake house, and took vacations in places I could only dream about as a struggling young attorney.

My friends and I listened to Bill and Angela's exploits, from their boats to their homes, from their children's accomplishments to their business successes. I recall numerous conversations at dinners and cocktail parties when all our wives were listening to Angela. Their eyes were misty with imagining how wonderful it would be to live her life. I used to watch the faces of the husbands as Bill bragged. Their eyes never left the ground, because they felt they should have been able to provide these same luxuries for their own families. Many of us forgot to cherish our own experiences as we envied Bill and Angela.

Over time, we all began to feel the beginnings of resentment. People raised by working parents usually assimilate an ethic that says you have to work for what you get, you get what you earn, and what you take for granted, you lose. The newlywed Campbells' lifestyle seemed to defy those basic truths.

If they had been smart enough to strike out on their own and establish boundaries as a couple, perhaps they might have made it. I've seen this happen once or twice, but success is rare.

Soon after marrying into wealth, the "pauper" spouse gets used to having money. Wealth is a narcotic, hooking those who experience it with the engaging lifestyle of the super-rich. Soon Bill and Angela became members at the country club, the tennis club, and the seaside yacht club, hobnobbing with the elite at every social event. Bill started bragging to his buddies about a work week of Monday through Friday, from 10:00 a.m. to 3:00 p.m., with every Thursday off for golf.

The couple rarely spent time with their old friends on the weekends, because the Campbell extended family was always involved in one grand affair or another. Like expensive luggage, Bill—the in-law—was pulled along on the family's travels . . . at no charge, of course. Somewhere down the road, Bill started to question his value in the eyes of his wife and children. His insecurity led to more boasting, which caused Bill to become more isolated from his friends, thus increasing his feelings of inadequacy. The vicious cycle continued, and after three years and several more kids, the stage was set for disaster.

## ENTERING THE VORTEX

Bill was a competent, hard worker, so Dad Campbell promoted him to the position of company president (primarily because the rest of the family never showed up). He became heavily involved with the financial business of the family, directing the family attorney, accountant, estate planner, and other financial advisers.

Soon the remainder of the family recognized Bill had the approval of their father and was slowing gaining control of the family empire. Another force of human nature surfaced in response: sibling rivalry. Unfortunately, when "blood family" senses a threat from the intruding in-law, they can assemble quickly and purposefully, like a pack of wolves.

For the first time—or at least the first time in a long time—Mom and Dad Campbell watched their children come together to discuss business issues and family concerns, exhibiting sincere interest in the family enterprise. In reality, the Campbell siblings were scheming about how to deal with Bill.

Like a deer in an open field, Bill never saw the members of the family circling around him. Over the next few months, each family member verbalized misgivings about Bill's actions in the company to Dad and Mom Campbell, raising doubt about his motives in controlling the family business. This synchronized symphony of suspicion comes naturally to siblings of wealth when their territory is threatened. Even the most detached or uninvolved family member suddenly comes up with eloquent commentary about family values and the need to carefully manage the family's wealth for the future. This development is often erroneously perceived by the parents as baby steps toward assuming authority.

Dad and Mom Campbell were proud. Parents in this scenario don't want to discourage this newfound camaraderie in their family, and if the only action necessary to appease the concerns of their children is to sacrifice their in-law, the decision is simple. In the Campbells' case, Bill was expendable.

## THE SPOUSE TAKES SIDES

Stop for a moment to focus on Angela. Wouldn't you expect her to come to Bill's rescue? After all, she married Bill and was raising a young family with him. But her friends and family had begun to undermine Angela's relationship with her husband. "Bill didn't earn his position." "He's always looking for a handout." "It's your money, right?"

Angela brushed off their comments at first, but eventually her kids began to fall victim to the vicious rumors and cutting remarks. Society is often cruel and unforgiving. People seek to level the playing field, even if there are undeserving casualties. Angela began to tell Bill, "You need to make a greater effort to get along with my family." Her implication was clear. Bill didn't count as "family" anymore. The price of admission to the family had changed; he had to be a blood relative. The grandchildren were welcome, but Bill was treated as an intruder.

Relations between Bill and Angela began to deteriorate, and Bill was slowly excluded from family affairs. Covertly, the family moved Angela's parents, siblings, and children onto one side and placed Bill on the other. The pack of wolves devoured Bill, offering condolences to Angela and extending a welcome arm to the children.

## A WORD OF WARNING

Let me offer a hard and fast boundary to protect marriages involving wealth: Be very reticent to work for your in-laws. As I reminisce over the past thirty years, I can recall countless individuals who have run or managed the companies or businesses of their super-rich in-laws. They make up a veritable graveyard of adverse outcomes and strained marriages.

My wife and I ran into Bill at a breakfast diner. After fifteen years of marriage and a nasty divorce, he was unshaven, wearing a rumpled white T-shirt and tattered beach sandals. He looked like a bum. His spirits were dim. We talked for a few moments about his kids, who were away with "the family" on a cruise.

He lived in a small two-bedroom apartment in a very modest part of town just down the street from the diner. The second bedroom was for his kids; he saw them only every other weekend. Otherwise he lived alone. I think of Bill as a good guy who wandered into Willy Wonka's candy factory and drank so much chocolate from the waterfall he drowned.

"Aren't you going to ask me how I fared in the divorce?" Bill rolled his eyes with a gentle smirk on his face. He knew I didn't have to ask. At Dad Campbell's request, I had drafted Angela's prenuptial agreement.

If you are a person of modest means who has wandered into a family of fortune, take this sage advice. Love your spouse, and let him or her be responsible for every interaction with his or her wealthy family regarding financial issues. Never presume your spouse's wealth is your wealth. Try your best to live by your own means, and avoid employment in the in-law's family enterprise. You will experience the joy of achieving your own goals, your spouse will respect you and your efforts, and your children will grow up in the presence of a model of solid character and integrity.

# CHAPTER EIGHT

# BITTER FAMILY BATTLES

Sylvia was his fifth wife.

Elliott Frederick's three children spent most of their lives putting up with their father's marital choices. Their natural mother, Elliott's first wife, had divorced him for philandering long before Elliott became wealthy. She lived in a modest house, which she paid for by working as a secretary for a local real estate broker. Her relationship with her children couldn't have been more heartfelt and sincere. Mom did not cause or retain significant animosity by jumping ship early in her marital career. She hadn't married him for his money.

Unfortunately, from Elliott's second wife onward, his money drew women like a magnet. Each time he brought a new wife into the family circle, the children grudgingly tolerated her obvious ulterior motive for marrying Elliott. By wife number four, the kids angrily refused to allow Elliott's grandchildren to call her "Grandma."

Immediately after marrying him, number five focused on ensuring her future upon Elliott's death. Sadly, at the age of seventy-five, Elliott was beginning to slip mentally and typically agreed with the person he had spoken to most recently. In fact, he met Sylvia when she served him breakfast in a local diner. After a few weeks, she'd convinced him he couldn't live without her. Elliott craved attention, and Sylvia was happy to provide it.

She quickly restricted Elliott's access to his children. Then she hired an estate-planning lawyer to redo Elliott's family trust, making her the beneficiary of the family business and several of the oceanfront properties. The total package she negotiated was worth between $50 and $60 million.

## ENTER THE LAWYERS

Nine times out of ten, family battles among the super-rich are fought over money. In general, conflict increases in direct proportion to the amount of wealth involved. Sons, daughters, brothers, and sisters become willing to destroy family relationships as acceptable casualties in pursuit of victory. By the way, I do not include simple arguments or disagreements in my definition of "family battles." True family battles escalate into full-blown court cases, with law firms fighting for each side, airing the family's dirty laundry in public.

At the time of Elliott's marriage to Sylvia, his oldest son, Scott, had served as president of the family business for twenty-seven years. When he asked to see a copy of the new trust, the family lawyer replied he had been specifically instructed not to share the trust. Scott met with his siblings, and together they hired an attorney to investigate.

The super-rich always hire the best—and most expensive—litigating lawyers. As a rule, lawyers gain their reputations by winning cases. Scott, his siblings, and Sylvia entered the boxing ring expecting a sure victory regardless of the cost. Large law firms of this ilk pride themselves on being "billing machines." Monthly invoices on each side commonly add up to more than $100,000, and triple that amount during the trial. The super-rich are perfect clients. Each side is headstrong and unwilling to compromise. I've often heard them exercising bragging rights at cocktail parties: "My lawyers are killing me. They've billed me over $2 million so far, and they tell me we haven't finished investigating yet."

After two years and more than $5 million in attorney's fees, not to mention the depositions of twenty-six witnesses and every family member, the lawyers were no closer to resolving the dispute than they had been in the beginning. Elliott's children didn't have the legal right to see the trust. All of the lawyers knew it. Sylvia knew it. End of game . . . until Sylvia became too greedy.

Sylvia fired Scott without severance, giving her son, Greg, presidency of the company. He fired all the other family members to ensure loyalty. However, his previous career as a real estate agent hadn't begun to prepare him to master the ins and outs of an international manufacturing company specializing in high-tech airplane- and rocket-engine components. The business suffered.

Elliott's children retained the same lawyers and sued Sylvia again. This time they added wrongful termination of employment and fraud to the suit because Elliott had promised his oldest son the right to buy the company upon his death. During the trial, Elliott's dementia revealed itself, as did Sylvia's role as his puppeteer. She coached Elliott to show up and deliver his lines. He couldn't. Each day in front of the jury, he tried to recall what had happened . . . and each day he told a different story.

The jury watched the machinations of a greedy fifth wife and called her on it. They found Scott's story compelling and awarded him $32 million in damages against his father. Sylvia refused to accept the game was over. She plunged her new spouse into bankruptcy to protect what little she still could take from him. Not until she had destroyed fifty years of good credit and negotiated about $10 million for herself did she let the rest go to Elliott's son and family.

Elliott has not seen any of his family since the day of the final court ruling. They don't know where he is, if he is still married to Sylvia, or even if he is still living.

## FALSE SECURITY

Money provides a counterfeit sense of security. It represents what we can have and what we won't have to do without. If we have money in the bank, it is less likely we will worry about the cost of food for our families. If we have a little more money in the bank, we may have the right to buy a house. Notice I mentioned the "right" to buy a house. Home ownership is not a "need." A rented home or apartment satisfies the same need for shelter. As we exercise our right to buy a house, we take out a mortgage. Now we "need" to pay the mortgage. To feel secure in a home and not risk losing it to the bank, we are required to make the mortgage payment. But remember, we are only contractually required to make the mortgage payment. It is always possible to sell the house and rent a place to live.

Now add a car, a second car, gasoline, plasma-screen televisions bought on credit, a loan for a swimming pool, a retirement savings account, college tuition for our children, medical insurance, and even a vacation home. Every time we exercise our right to acquire something else we want but don't necessarily need, we increase the financial requirements for maintaining that lifestyle. Wants become needs.

As we acquire, our feet lift off the ground. The more we acquire, the further we move from reality. Before long, we are so far off course we cannot determine what we can do without. We lose sight of the basic priorities of sustenance, family, and spirituality. Eventually, we might even worry more about maintaining a vacation home than about the future educational costs for our children.

How does this principle apply to the super-rich? They are so accustomed to all of the "wants" they have acquired they don't isolate individual items any longer. The cost of their lifestyle is enormous. Add the children of the super-rich to the recipe and a second generation starts life with their feet high above the ground. They don't have any idea about what life's terrain looks like. They have never experienced "need." They only know "want."

Unlike the rest of us, financial security isn't an issue or a goal for the super-rich—until someone tries to take it away. Only then do they imagine what it might be like to do without "wants," not to mention needs. Generally, when family members attack each other, the stakes are high and the fear of losing financial security can border on hysteria. A divorcing spouse will do everything he or she can to take a good chunk of the fortune. Add a couple of bad marriages, and the costs become exponential. Even someone with a personal fortune of $100 million is at risk. Family battles begin when the super-rich become aware of that risk . . . usually for the first time.

## THE SPOILS OF WAR

Joe's grandfather pioneered the idea of offering low-priced electronics to the public. He was a stern, frugal man, epitomizing America's classic entrepreneur. During much of his lifetime, the family business was in growth mode. The children were raised modestly, with good family values. At a typical holiday gathering, a table for thirty-five people extended from the family dining room into an area of the grandparents' home built specifically to accommodate the extended family. Laughter and banter over the economy, politics, and more filled the room.

An undercurrent of thankfulness always seasoned Grandpa's

words. He repeatedly declared, "Never take these blessings for granted. Everything can be taken away. We need to appreciate every minute of this family's success. This wasn't my accomplishment. The Almighty gave this to our family, and He expects us to be good stewards of our gift."

The children and grandchildren weren't completely sure how the family's fortune had been made, but they were well-versed in the fact it could be taken away at any time. They heard it daily.

One day Grandpa died. His two sons, Ed and Frank, took over the business, and they had very different ideas about how the business should be positioned for the future. But Grandpa continued to receive credit for the company's success and origin. The generational leash was still attached.

The sons decided to split the company into two areas of concentration, with one side marketing and selling products directly to the public and the other marketing and selling products through retailers and distributors.

In our society's growing preference for disintermediation, or "cutting out the middleman," the older son, Joe's father, Ed, proved to be more successful. His side of the business boarded a rocket and went vertical. Within ten years, the other side of the business failed, and Frank's side of the family returned to ordinary means, as did his children and grandchildren.

Ed, his wife, Margaret, and their four children flourished. The holiday table looked much the same as it had in Grandpa's days, except for the obvious omission of the other side of the family. Frank and his children no longer attended, because it was too difficult for them to witness the reality of what they had lost. In addition, they were deeply hurt by what they perceived to be Ed's heartless neglect of Grandpa's example. They had expected familial loyalty to be more important than business success. But they were wrong.

Ed's adult children all worked in the company and lived handsome lifestyles. Ed groomed his eldest son, Joe, as the heir apparent to run the company. However, when Joe was just twenty-five years old, Ed unexpectedly died, leaving Margaret as the head of the family and Joe at the helm of the company. The business grew steadily for twenty-five more years. Joe benefited more than the other children, who were now in their fifties. He was secretive about the operations and financial condition of the company.

Family gatherings were still large and festive, but Joe never mentioned his grandfather or modeled an attitude of gratitude. He believed he alone was responsible for the success of the company and overtly conveyed his belief that his siblings were lucky he kept them on the payroll. Tensions grew.

As Joe's mother, Margaret, entered her retirement years, he took the liberty of preparing her taxes, paying her expenses, and giving her enough money to prevent her from asking questions about the company. Later, when he approached her, insisting she sell him the company at a price substantially less than what the family thought the business was worth, Margaret recoiled and refused. Livid, Joe quit, vowing to destroy the family's company.

He started his own enterprise and began to steal away customers who had grown loyal to him over the past twenty-five years. Joe filed a lawsuit for fraud against his mother, insisting he had been wrongfully terminated and denied his right to own the company. The family quickly became polarized; Joe, his wife, and his children took one side, and Margaret and the rest of three generations stood on the other. The battle raged for years. Margaret was emotionally crushed.

Holiday dinners continued minus one of the families. The woman at the head of the table was heartbroken. Joe's family lost their uncles, aunts, cousins, and grandmother. He cinched the noose of pride around his neck and dedicated the rest of his life to bitterness.

The company survived, the family reunited with the long-estranged members of Frank's extended family to fight against Joe, and the family created ghosts . . . ghosts of the brisk talks and walks that followed a hearty family meal and ghosts of gratefulness for the family's good fortune. What would Grandpa think?

Family battles are not unique to the super-rich. But the super-rich have their own special brand. The stakes are higher, and they have the resources to sustain disputes over longer periods of time.

Also, the battles that occur among average families usually involve direct confrontation. One family member confronts another and expresses his anger, disappointment, or hurt. Most often these are mere skirmishes and resolve quickly. They are healthy for maturing families and necessary for all to feel heard and valued.

On the contrary, the super-rich often choose finances over family. Fighting over money begins on a level playing field.

After all, everyone in the family of the super-rich feels entitled to part of the wealth. What the super-rich forget is victory requires an attack. The victor who gains the spoils leaves the vanquished . . . and the vanquished no longer want to be part of the family.

# PART THREE

## LIVING BEHIND CASTLE WALLS

# CHAPTER NINE

# PRETEND FRIENDS

Once you have discovered who the real friends of the super-rich are, it would be an act of kindness to explain it to them. They would like to know too.

Friendship—genuine friendship—is an irreplaceable gift. In a sense, friendship acts to level the valleys of the human experience, filling in the potholes of everyday life. A sincere friend accepts you as you are, in spite of your flaws. They offer companionship and comfort, acting as a sort of emotional scanner that can identify your undisclosed hurts and desires. Genuine friends are assets who help you overcome and forget the negative and rejoice in the positive. Life is not meant to be lived alone.

## A LONELY WORLD

Barbara is the heir to a fortune acquired through a brilliant product invented by her father. He was barely able to provide for his family as a worker for Bethlehem Steel. But one day he imagined and built a device that would increase the flow of coolant to any machine that required constant temperature reduction. In simple terms, his invention was the first computerized version of an automobile radiator, and it offered a multitude of applications that eventually ranged from machine shops to nuclear power generators. At the end of her father's life the company sold for hundreds of millions of dollars. Barbara inherited the fortune with her brother.

When Barbara asked me to be her family's legal counsel, we had a frank discussion. I told her straight up, "I am not being paid to be your friend. I am being paid to protect you, to be open and honest, and to be incredibly candid with my thoughts at all times." I almost got fired before I was hired.

Barbara grew up in a middle-class neighborhood, but she had all kinds of friends. However, once she assumed the mantle of wealth, the quality of her friendships changed. She is an insightful woman: "I have old friends and new friends. My old friends fit into two categories: the ones who liked me before I inherited money and still do, and the ones who liked me before I inherited money and now like my money more than me. The new friends," she continued, "also fit into two categories: those who want something from me, and those who have received something from me and want more." She has a wonderfully "edgy" sense of humor.

At least Barbara gets to retain twenty-five percent of her friends. Consider those who were born with wealth. They are left with the last two categories; they rarely have friendships without strings attached.

## ULTERIOR MOTIVES

When Barbara throws a party it is always a spectacular event with concert pianists or small ensembles, lavish dinners, famous chefs, party gifts, dancing, and every kind of fun imaginable. She spares no expense to be sure everyone has a great time.

At one of her beautiful parties, Barbara met an earnest prison warden who had dedicated his life to serving the inmates of one of America's most notorious prisons. His credibility was heightened by his lifelong commitment to his faith. Barbara is a devout Christian, and she has a generous heart.

After the party, the warden immediately became Barbara's close friend. He was at her disposal for any need. She soon professed he was an "honest friend interested only in me." I heard it often: "He tells me he loves me," she declared with pride.

At one point, one of Barbara's friends was incarcerated for a nonviolent crime. At Barbara's request, the warden went into action immediately. He was terrific. He knew the "ins" and "outs" of the system. He knew the procedure for the incarceration of an inmate and what the new inmate would experience during his first days and weeks in the prison. His friendship was valuable and comforting for the inmate's family and for Barbara.

Several months later, the warden called Barbara and asked for $100,000 to support a business venture. Barbara called me in tears, devastated by her overestimation of a blossoming friendship and the unexpected revelation of the warden's ulterior motives. He may have begun the relationship with sincerity. However, after being around someone of such substantial financial means, he began to see Barbara as a resource rather than as a relationship. Before long, such friends are not shy about asking for whatever they want. The relational dynamic constantly changes.

I hear stories like these all the time. Understandably, insincere relationships harden the hearts of the rich, make them cynical toward approaching strangers, and basically sentence them to life in a fortified castle whose drawbridge is seldom lowered in welcome.

## UNINTENDED SEPARATION

Once you begin to acquire, others begin to admire. And when people admire, they covet. When they covet, they usually begin to manipulate and angle for what they want. The chasm widens from both directions. The haves seek to protect themselves from the rest. The super-rich often feel sure others are trying to get what they have. This protectiveness leads them to avoid people of seemingly lesser means. As they do so, they appear to be arrogant and condescending. Many of the rich intentionally cultivate the impression they do not want anything we can offer, either materially or emotionally. We don't have anything to exchange for their attention, favor, or friendship.

For the have nots, this aloof attitude undermines the desire to connect and be friends with the haves. Who wants to befriend someone who makes us feel bad? The gap grows wider, and the inability of the two groups to relate increases. The super-rich unintentionally—or sometimes intentionally—lose the opportunity to receive and give friendship.

The wealthy would like nothing more than for us to like them for who they are. Unfortunately, they struggle to clearly define who they really are because they haven't been challenged or genuinely encouraged because of their status and position. The rich share the fate of many celebrities, who often thirst for real friendship.

My wife and I spent a week vacationing at a campground near the ocean. Our group included ten families of various socioeconomic means. We arrived as acquaintances and left as friends. The people were genuine, but I found it very interesting to consider why people of little means are so much more willing to reach out to others than those who have more. My wife labeled this phenomenon as a "clash of expectations." Those of modest backgrounds have realistic expectations for one another; they are open and willing to reach out to strangers. They easily establish friendships that become the source of much fun and fulfillment. Rich people tend to be very leery of other people; every introduction or gesture of friendship is met with intense scrutiny.

This distinction can occur even when the disparity in economic levels is modest. The Chadwicks, a super-wealthy family, joined the campers for the first time that year. The dad hired a service to set up the entire trailer in the park, complete with tables, awnings, and bedding. Their campsite was like a mobile home, complete with air conditioning and a misting sprayer on the patio. When he was ready to leave, the service came and picked it up. He only had to pile his kids in the accompanying car and leave.

He and his family participated in many of the activities, but with an air of reservation that suggested they hadn't yet bought into this "lesser" form of vacationing. Half of the families were in awe of him, and the other half resented him for bringing his entitled mind-set to their very modest and prized campout. It was readily apparent he and his family didn't fully appreciate the simplicity of the long-standing traditional campout. When the children created skits to perform for the parents around the campfire at night, the Chadwick children didn't participate because they were accustomed not to entertaining but to being entertained. Their actions unintentionally reminded everyone else they were financially elevated.

The Chadwicks' overall intentions were probably good, but they isolated themselves by living on a different economic level than the rest. I'm not sure they even realized it.

## FRIENDS DURING A FALL?

A benefit I attended attracted some of California's richest supporters. The silent auction at the beginning was followed by a fabulous dinner, and the evening concluded with a live auction that historically brought in the lion's share of fund-raising dollars for the event. On that particular night, a strange tension lingered in the air.

Carolyn, a beautiful forty-something woman dressed in a couture Escada gown, served as the chairwoman and our hostess. Her husband, Frank, was a prominent hedge-fund manager. They were some of our area's wealthiest residents.

Although the Wall Street Journal had not yet printed the story, Carolyn's "friends" had already betrayed her trust, spreading rumors that Frank's fund had recently plummeted and sought protection in bankruptcy court. His other ventures were tied up in bank guarantees made possible by his portion of ownership in the hedge fund and their other assets. The banks had spent the week in federal court tying up Frank and Carolyn's assets, including their enormous beachfront home.

Near the close of the evening, Carolyn stood up and excitedly announced the items that had been donated for the auction. She reminded the guests a papillon puppy would be available and mentioned she hoped it would bring in a donation near $25,000.

At that moment, I heard one woman at my table lean over to another and say, "Wouldn't you be a little embarrassed to stand up there and ask for money if you were almost broke yourself? Don't you think she is being a little presumptuous?" The whispered answer came quickly, "Maybe she should auction off her dress. She won't need it for much longer."

In the span of a week, Frank and Carolyn fell from the highest rung on the social ladder to become the latest dirt to hit the tabloids.

## GENUINE FRIENDSHIP

The first generation of the super-rich typically retain some genuine friends—the people who knew them before they became wealthy. But subsequent generations rarely find friends without ulterior motives. The real connections they make are usually with people who don't have the means to compete with them or anything to gain from them. They often meet friends like these in unexpected places and develop close relationships outside of their normal, everyday lives.

My father cultivated an unusual friendship with a very wealthy man whose name is recognizable worldwide. They met when they were young, and their friendship lasted because Dad didn't care one bit about his friend's money. I remember walking into my dad's office and seeing this man sitting on the couch with his feet up and a soda in his hand. They spent hours shooting the breeze. Dad listened and spoke the truth as he saw it.

One afternoon, this man confided that no one else in his life would tell him the truth. "How am I supposed to know if I'm out of line? Or if I do something well?" My father was brutally honest with him about his career, his kids, and his life. It was amazing to watch the grin spread over this celebrity's face when he spent time with Dad. People just didn't talk to him that way. The interaction was always a sincere pleasure for both. He had no other outlet for candid and truthful honesty. It would be a sad, lonely way to live.

What about your friends? I'm willing to bet most of them don't like you based on the car you drive or the dinners you might buy. They like you because you are funny, because you are kind, because you are talented, or just because you are you.

Your true friends are invaluable assets. You can trust them. They will stand up for you. True friends will fight for your personal cause, and especially for you as a person. Most important, they serve as a litmus test of your character. When you are out of line, they will tell you. When you are successful—even moderately—they will cheer you on. Cherish your friends.

# CHAPTER TEN

# UNRELENTING COMPETITION

For several years I had the privilege of serving on the board of directors of an international organization with about twenty of this country's richest families. At least two of the board members were billionaires. We became acquaintances. I was invited to join the board because of my skills as an attorney. Otherwise, this poker table's stakes were way too high for me.

One weekend, one of the board members invited me to his home in Palm Springs. He collected cars as a hobby. When I arrived, he showed me his Duesenberg, two Ferraris, a Rolls Royce, and two Shelby Cobras.

When lunchtime came, an award-winning French chef who had been lured away from a world-class restaurant cooked us this man's favorite meal, gourmet hamburgers and home-made french fries. I can't begin to describe what it was like to eat burgers off of Limoges china in a dining room filled with $3 million of furniture and artwork.

The LPGA's Dinah Shore golf tournament was being played

that weekend on the course near his house. The management had closed the course for the week to make sure it remained perfect for the upcoming tournament, but they invited us to play the course alone that afternoon. What a treat!

While we enjoyed our round, my new friend told me about an upcoming event, an annual party in the desert for the richest of the rich. He sounded bored at the thought of attending, but he mentioned he had to go because his wife was a co-chair.

He explained everyone in the area always clamored for an invitation, but only a select few would be invited. The guest list was comprised of four "thirds." Yes; in spite of Euclidian geometry, four thirds made a whole for this party. The first third was comprised of the super-rich couples who were invited every year. The second third typically included famous people like former United States presidents, congressmen, CEOs of Fortune 500 companies, best-selling authors, and movie producers . . . but no celebrities. The third group included the "new" money in town. These guinea pigs were under examination. Would they qualify to join the "in crowd?" Or were they just passing through?

The makeup of the fourth third caught my attention. These people were the exclusive subject of conversation, and yet they would not be in attendance. This uninvited group had fallen from grace because of a change in their financial statements or, even better, a scandal. This non-attending third became the entertainment for the evening. They were admired for their courage, apologetically excused for their misfortune, and generally barbecued as the main course.

## CHASING THE EXTRAORDINARY

Rich people appear to have much in common. They can afford what others can't. They like expensive things. They travel to exotic places others don't even recognize. They control almost everything they see. However, they tend to run in the same circles and experience the same things over and over again.

As a result, rich people are often very eccentric. I know many people who cloak themselves in peculiarity in order to sidestep the possibility of comparison. For instance, Linda requires her personal assistant to review the seating arrangements for every public event she attends. The process includes hours of taking and poring over photographs of Linda lookalikes sitting in each chair at the suggested table so she can select the best lighting, view, and arrangement. If the event planner or host refuses to play ball with her, she won't attend. Because she is a big draw, event organizers usually bow to Linda's demands.

Besides their eccentricities, the rich also seek new thrills. The ordinary is dismissed as mundane and passé. I believe the rich often have aversion to everyday life because it reminds them they are ordinary on the inside. Once they are wealthy, the last thing their egos can handle is seeming average again.

Jim's vice is yacht racing on Lake Arrowhead in California. He owns the sleekest, most expensive boat on the market, and he pays an entire crew to keep it in top shape. Every weekend, he joins his yacht club on the water and sails to his heart's content . . . and to win every race.

One weekend, I joined Jim and a group of friends at his

lakefront estate. Early Saturday morning, we all trundled outside to watch the weekly race. A new guy showed up with a
top-of-the-line boat. I could tell Jim wasn't happy about it. "He
joined the club last month. I haven't seen his stuff yet, but he
looks like an arrogant fool," Jim muttered under his breath, roll-
ing his eyes.

Sure enough, as the race began the new challenger crept up
on Jim's boat. At the last turn, the newcomer cut Jim off, causing his boat to lose speed. The interloper won the race. Jim was
livid. "He cheated! Cheated!" We had to physically hold him
back from accosting the other guy.

At dinner that night, Jim swore he would ram the other
boat if the other man ever tried to pull another stunt like that
again. We brushed his words off with laughter, daring him
to try.

I didn't think another thing about it. But a friend of mine
called me the following Saturday. "Well, Jim actually did it."

"Did what?"

"He rammed the guy's boat! Don't you remember? When
the new guy made the turn and tried to cut Jim off, he just
slammed his whole boat right into the middle of the other one.
Both boats sunk like stones. When we pulled everyone out
of the water, Jim couldn't stop laughing. He wrote the guy a
$150,000 check to pay for the boat and told him not to try that
again or he'd do the exact same thing."

I signed off. Jim's boat probably cost a quarter of a million dollars. That's $400,000 at the bottom of Lake Arrowhead
just because Jim didn't want to lose. He literally blew away his

competition . . . and loved it. The competitors, as well as their families, have not spoken since.

## WINNING THE INVISIBLE GAME

Many of the rich struggle to find a place of refuge where they can relax and be themselves. When they spend time with other wealthy people, they are pulled into a metaphorical game of chess. There is no "draw." You either win or lose at each encounter. The wins are temporary and the losses offensive.

Because of my job, I often spend time at functions for the wealthy. These parties and benefits are strikingly similar, so I tend to observe those around me throughout the evening. Most conversations between super-rich people follow a specific pattern.

One person usually begins with some claim to fame. I call this "boundary staking" because it reminds me of an animal in the wild defining its territory. Both parties begin to drop names or identify the charities they support. This royal cockfighting escalates quickly into something plainly pedantic and boastful. Onlookers like me become tense and feel themselves taking deep breaths. This ritualistic dance usually concludes with submission by one to the other or, more commonly, a mutual conclusion that they do not agree and are therefore from different camps. Unfortunately, these camps typically have populations of one.

A common conversation sounds like this:

"What causes do you support?"

"My wife and I share our time and dollars with the local Performing Arts Center. We serve on the board and are members of the Benefactors Group." This piece of information signals a donation of $1 million or more. Impressive.

The first person must fold or raise the bet. If he chooses to fold, he will make small talk and then saunter toward the outer reaches of the cocktail party.

If he is a financial hitter, he will raise the bet: "That's wonderful. We just had the privilege of participating and contributing to the new expansion of Hoag Hospital. Have you toured the new Halloway Cancer Center?" This also requires a donation of $1 million. Volley returned.

The ball bounces back into the other person's court. It's time for his best game. "As a matter of fact, we have always felt Hoag is one of our region's finest facilities."

"My name is Nathan Halloway. My family built the Halloway Cancer Center as a tribute to my mother, who is a breast cancer survivor." Game . . . Set . . . Match.

A comeback from this type of assault is rare. More important, the first person will never forget Nathan Halloway's name and will brag about having met him at the next soiree.

Behold the food chain of the rich.

## STAYING OFF THE PLAYING FIELD

The games rich people play aren't always fun. Expectations are high. Even the most amazing accomplishments and experiences can always be topped by someone else. More is rarely enough. Respect is earned one moment and dissolved the next.

Be thankful you are free to increase and decrease according to your own effort. You can become well-read and converse with friends and strangers. You don't strike fear or stimulate envy in the hearts of others. You are flawed. You may know a lot about politics but not be able to carry a tune. You may be "Stevie Wonder" on the piano but have two left feet when it comes to dancing. You can move in a variety of social and economic circles without fear. You can receive an invitation to a party and attend with confidence that your presence is desired for your own sake, not for the "entertainment" you might provide. You have the opportunity to be your own person.

# CHAPTER ELEVEN

# INEVITABLE ALIENATION

Pets—dogs, cats, birds, rats, or even tarantulas—often become surrogates for human companionship. They can bring comfort, offer loyalty, and be summoned whenever we want them. If you crave the kind of companionship a tarantula brings, you can pull it out of its cage and let it crawl all over you; when you're finished, you can return it to the cage. Most people have pets as an adjunct to their family activities; for instance, the dog is a part of the daily family routine, doubling as a horse, tackle dummy, pool toy, television pillow, and more. The typical family order is spouse, children, and pet.

Priorities are quite different in the mansion on the bluff. Pets of the rich often occupy a different position in the home: self, pet, spouse, and children. In affluent communities, dogs are a badge of honor, a sign of wealth. The more expensive and rare the breed, the more wealthy and cultured the owner is perceived to be. The owner only owns and loves the dog. The maid walks, feeds, bathes, and manages the dog.

To my knowledge, the communities where my clients live

do not boast a single mutt. On the rare occasion when a dog is walked by the owner, he or she will typically stop passersby to recite the pedigree and the lineage of the dog. If you have never heard of the breed, the owner gets bonus points, especially among the super-rich. Their goal is simple: my dog is better than your dog.

## A SOURCE OF LOVE AND ACCEPTANCE

An elderly acquaintance of mine passed away, leaving four grown children and nine grandchildren. When her will was made public, she left less than $100,000 to each of her children, nothing to her grandchildren, and $73 million to her pet poodle. She arranged for the canine's care until its death and then placed the rest of the money in a trust to care for the gravesite in perpetuity.

Behind this display of obsessive-compulsive love is a painful history of family division, caused by the twin oppressors of wealth and greed. When the patriarch of the family died, the mother fought off her children's greedy attempts to extort money from her for years. She lost their love and affection, so she fell into a serious mistake that is made by too many wealthy matriarchs: She bought her children. She started with automobiles, then houses, and eventually moved into annual disbursements.

Her dialogue with her children always started out with flowery speeches in which they expressed concern for her day, health, and more. However, every conversation ended with a request for more money. Eventually she began to screen her calls, avoiding her children altogether.

The children began to get angry, gossiping among themselves about what a selfish woman their mother had become. They stopped calling, except when they had a real financial emergency.

Far too often I've witnessed the plight of people who allow their success to be measured by material things and then lose the love of their families as a result. True, it is usually the individual's fault, but the pain is still real and deep. My client's children were busy with their own kids and lives, so perhaps the bitterness was less predominant in their everyday lives. But the woman thought about the rift all day, every day. Her pain was continuous.

She turned to her dog for unconditional love and acceptance. It spent as much time with her as she liked. It never complained. It never asked for money. When she died, her last act was a reflection of her loneliness and isolation. Though it seems sinister and vengeful at first glance, consider her desperation. She screamed from the grave, "I am lonely! I die in pain!"

Her children did not attend her funeral. Even worse, her grandchildren never knew their grandmother. If she had given all of her money to the dog ten years earlier, leaving her poor and needy, she might have had a chance with her own children. The last years of her life were as isolated and cold as the grave she now occupies.

## LEAVING A LEGACY

My grandmother on my dad's side was called "Pokie." As I write her name, I am immediately called back to my childhood memories of a robust woman with open arms and eyes that crinkled at the corners. She unreservedly gave me her time and love. I remember reading Bible stories with Pokie every night I spent at her home. She fed me, corrected me, took care of me when I was sick, and listened when I laughed and when I cried. Her stories formed the foundation of an immovable faith. Her words of encouragement have echoed in my mind every week of my life. She believed in me when others doubted. She was my model and mentor.

I wonder if she would recognize the eating nook I built in my home to remind me of the endless afternoons I spent with her in Ohio, eating cookies and listening to her stories. Would she recognize the pieces of her nineteenth-century furniture that now occupy special places in my home? How would she feel if she knew the great-grandchildren she never met hope to own one of Pokie's antiques when I'm gone? Not because of their intrinsic value, but because they belonged to this legend in our family.

She died in 1980, but we talk about her today as if she had visited yesterday. Pokie died with a home worth around $50,000 and a retirement savings of less than $80,000. None of her grandchildren are upset with her because she couldn't buy each of us a car. She gave us life. She invested in our future by giving us her present.

When she died, each of her ten grandchildren received $1,000. We furnished the nursery of our first son with the money, in her honor. We told each of our three boys about the sacrifice Pokie made to bring joy to our family. The furniture has become an heirloom simply because it was connected to a special lady. She left an incredible legacy of love.

## AVOIDING ISOLATION

You probably believe you would remain the same if you suddenly acquired money. Why? The answer is obvious. You would never let money get in the way of your family. But think about it. Could you really stop it from interfering? Money, like a small stream, cuts a slow and deep path in rock. It creeps up on you.

What do you do when you are bored? Go for a walk? Call a friend? Play a sport you enjoy? Watch your favorite movie? Each of these activities puts you in the path of others who enrich your life because they bring variety and complexity. Others bring controversy, laughter, anger, tears, and conflict. After being with others for long periods of time, you may even enjoy a little time in isolation . . . but not for long.

You have to go to work tomorrow. You have to deal with others. They will cause you to compete, compromise, debate, argue, discuss, and cry. They will accept you and reject you. You may even have to try to get along with others.

When you don't have money, your friends are not a yo-yo on a string that comes back no matter what. Your friends are baseballs. If you take a swing at one, you may knock that friend out of the park; he or she is gone forever. But if you care for others and give them the real you, they will shower you with affection and love . . . for free.

I'll never forget Elizabeth Kennedy, the richest woman in my dad's tiny hometown of Poland, Ohio. To this day, I don't know how rich she really was, but her home used to be a college where President William McKinley attended law school.

Picture a small Midwestern town with a straight, sycamore-lined street running right through the middle of town. Twenty small houses sat on the left, side by side, and one long, black, wrought-iron fence trailed down on the right, enclosing a grassy park. A stately, century-old mansion sat right in the middle, complete with servants' quarters, a barn, and stables.

Because she lived directly across the street, my grand-mother knew Elizabeth as well as any of the regular folk in town. As a boy, I remember every time Elizabeth drove her car down the long cobblestone driveway, her servant, Billy, a gray-haired black man who had been with her for decades, walked alongside her car to open and close the gate. My grandfather or grandmother invariably commented, "Elizabeth is leaving." Then the other would reply, "I spoke with her yesterday. She said she was going to have her hair done in town for a party she is having at the mansion tonight."

As a youth, I didn't pay much attention, except to won-der why everyone always wanted to know Elizabeth Ken-nedy's business. Sometimes during supper, my grandparents and neighbors engaged in a duel to determine who knew the most about what Elizabeth was doing that day, tomorrow, next week, and so on. They talked about her as if she were royalty. In fact, she looked a little bit like England's Queen Elizabeth and dressed every day as though she were going to Sunday church.

I spent almost every summer in Poland, Ohio, with my grandparents. When I was thirteen, I worked for Elizabeth. I weeded her garden, fixed her barn doors, and even replaced a faucet inside her home. I couldn't understand why I became the focus of discussion for the entire town. "What does Elizabeth's house look like on the inside?" "Did you talk to her at all today?" "Does anyone come over to visit her?" "Did you fix the faucet in her private bathroom?" "What was it like?"

The mansion was quiet and empty. Whenever Billy called me into the house to fix something, Elizabeth was always sitting in the living room alone, reading a book. No one came to visit during the entire three months I worked there. Even though she often allowed me to work near her without saying a word, at other times she asked me about my family, my grandmother, our family dinners, our trips, passions, and what made us laugh. I sensed she hadn't heard laughter in her home for a long time.

On the day before I flew home to California, she told me she was going to miss me. She said her family did not visit her anymore: "They are just waiting for me to die." As a lad, I was shocked to hear of such disrespect, but I politely smiled because I couldn't think of anything to say.

Billy escorted me down the cobblestone driveway to open the gate for me one last time. He placed his hand on my shoulder as we strode down the lane. At the last moment, I turned and looked back at the mansion. Elizabeth stood on her front porch, partially obscured by the screen door. She was holding a handkerchief, and I could tell she was crying.

Across the street, in her little row house, my grandmother had already peeled potatoes and snapped green beans for dinner. When I got home, she was resting in the backyard on the patio with my grandfather and several friends who had just stopped by to chat. I joined the group, drank a glass of fresh-squeezed lemonade, and for an hour we laughed, and shared, and lived. I wish I'd invited Elizabeth to join us.

# CHAPTER TWELVE

# ARTIFICIAL INTELLIGENCE

Are the super-rich smarter than the rest of us? Think for a moment before you answer. You probably want to say, "Of course not." But if you're really honest your answer will probably be, "Yes, they are smarter." Why? Wealthy people are "smarter" because we say so. Regardless of the origin of their riches, the world looks at the wealthy and ordains them as knowing more than the average Joe. Based on the common assumption that wealth and intelligence are correlated, we naturally tend to want to believe the best of those who have acquired wealth.

It is true many entrepreneurs who have made fortunes inventing products and ideas may have been geniuses in their fields. But a PhD in chemistry shouldn't give a person license to provide counsel about child rearing, and a Grammy-winning voice doesn't entitle the super-rich to offer counsel on global warming. But we listen, don't we?

Historically, the rich ruled over the masses. They governed, judged, and sentenced the population according to their rules. We are used to giving them authority and power. Their opinions and desires take precedence over our own . . . because we allow them to do so. As a result, most of the super-rich expect to get their way, and we rarely prove them wrong.

The have nots are often reluctant to challenge the haves. We secretly want a sliver of their world and the prize of their friendship. Everyone puts on knee pads, kneels to the ground, and begins the process of canonizing the lucky person with the bucks.

In order to persuade rich people to invite us into their world, we generally have to submit to their rules. Picture a chihuahua that comes face to face with a German shepherd. Immediately, the smaller dog rolls over and shows its neck to the larger dog, showing submission in order to avoid a fight. In my experience, the rich often require the same type of acknowledgment. Granted, some are more subtle. But each has developed a set of entry requirements. They won't allow us in until they are satisfied we are willing to play the game their way.

## THE PETER PRINCIPLE

Greg was the son of a mega auto dealer who employed about three hundred people. Greg never finished high school. He preferred partying, fast cars, and motocross. After being unable to sustain several different attempts at gainful employment, Greg turned to his father, Ralph, for career guidance. In very short order, father and son were able to conclude Greg did not have the skill, aptitude, or passion for a "regular" job. His dad was sixty-four years old, Greg was thirty-four. Ralph was proud of having built four successful, large auto dealerships. He was also very proud of his only son. After all, Greg had become a well-known amateur motocross rider. With the eight motorcycles Greg had wrecked, he had won four county amateur championships. Ralph secretly believed all along his son would come into the car business when he was ready.

One afternoon, without much discussion, Ralph decided he would vacate his position as president; he would stop running all operations and allow Greg to step in and take the controls. Since Ralph was the sole shareholder, only one vote was required, and that vote was cast with confidence and pride. Presto! Greg was crowned and invited to take the throne. Ralph believed in trial by fire. But the fire and excitement he was feeling was his own, not Greg's.

Greg knew nothing about the car business. But he discovered one of the dealership's eighteen mechanics, Jim, was skilled and experienced in working on motocross bikes. Grooming a personal mechanic for his hobby became Greg's first order of business. Jim's new first priority was to keep Greg's bikes finely tuned and ready for use at any moment. The realization by the other mechanics that Jim no longer had to meet the hourly quota required of each of them immediately sent a chain reaction through the service department.

Only six months into his new position, Greg recognized the dealership could run itself. Each of the departments—sales, parts, service, and finance—had a manager who was quite skilled at administrating his position on the organizational chart. Between Greg's new passion for golf, to which he was

introduced by another dealer's son, and local motocross com-
petitions, Greg's weekday calendar was becoming full. What
Greg didn't recognize was that the heads of the four departments needed a boss also. There are inherent conflicts between
departments. The boss needs to set policy and mediate difficult overlaps in operations. Tacit wars broke out between the
departments at the dealership, fractionalizing the business into
four separate hostile camps, with each blaming the other for
what had become a steady loss in income for the dealership. No
one dared complain to Greg. The employees hated him already.
Surprisingly, when Ralph would appear each week to check on
morale, no one had the gumption to tell him what was going
on.

The Peter Principle was in play. The Peter Principle occurs
when a person in a chain of authority is elevated to a position
just beyond his or her ability or level of knowledge. In this case,
Greg was not only inexperienced; he was also absent much of
the time. Each employee would smile and tell Ralph his son
was slowly "getting a handle on the business." Everyone was
afraid except . . .

## THE KING HAS NO CLOTHES

Charlie, the "lot boy," was a middle-aged African American
man with a family of six. The lot boy was in charge of washing the cars. Not only was the title "lot boy" demeaning, it
also identified the person who received the least respect and

wielded the least amount of power in the business. If the managers needed someone to run for a bag of hamburgers for lunch, Charlie jumped in a truck and sped from the parking lot to the nearest fast-food joint.

Charlie kept six-hundred cars freshly washed and sparkling every day. He worked under the direction of the service manager's assistant, who reported to the service manager, who reported to the service director, who reported to the general manager, who was supposed to report to Greg. The washing area was located at the rear of the ten-acre facility. Charlie moved the cars from the front line to the wash bays and back to the front storage lot twelve hours a day, seven days a week. At the time, this was the typical practice at most auto agencies.

If you had asked Charlie who decided it was best to wash the cars in the wash bays in the rear of the dealership, he would have said he was following the direction of the assistant service manager. Then if you asked, "Why do you think he knows best, Charlie?" He would have responded, "He's done this before and knows best."

Each employee in the chain of command followed the direction of his or her superior. If they had been asked the same question, they likely would have given the same basic answer: "My manager knows best."

Ralph was a humble man. He used to speak with everyone at the business; his employees loved and respected him greatly. One of his favorite things to ask each employee was, "How do you think your job should be done?"

Ralph's office had been in the rear of the facility, close to the wash bays. He greeted Charlie every morning. On one of his visits to the Honda dealership he asked Charlie, "How would you do your job if it were up to you?"

Charlie cleverly responded, "I would wash the cars the way the assistant manager told me to wash them."

Ralph was not so easily appeased. "Charlie, I'm serious. If you were in charge of this job [which he actually was, whether he realized it or not], what could we do to improve the process?"

Charlie lit up like a Christmas tree. He had little interaction with Greg and was anxious to contribute. He knew the business of washing cars. "Well," Charlie said, "you realize moving six hundred cars from the front of the lot to the rear, three times a week, results in a lot of fender benders and scrapes? That costs you more than a little money, Mr. Ralph. And after we wash the cars, we have to let them dry awhile before we towel them off, which prevents us from bringing in the next half dozen cars. I like to target two hundred and fifty cars a day. We wash the whole inventory every two and a half days, just often enough to keep them from looking dusty again. Oh, and one more thing. We leave the cars running while they are being washed, which uses hundreds of gallons of gas every month."

"So what is the solution, Charlie?" Ralph kept pushing.

Charlie hesitated for a few seconds—glancing around as if someone might be listening—and then he turned back to Ralph. In a whisper he said, "Don't move the cars." Then he pleaded, "But don't tell the assistant service manager I said anything."

Within two weeks, Ralph assisted Greg in hiring the installation of underground plumbing in the front car lot with hose faucets every hundred feet. Charlie washed the cars right where they sat, saving thousands of dollars in gas and protecting the inventory.

The following month, Ralph drove on the lot again and smiled at Charlie with approval and pride. "By the way, Charlie, are there any other ideas you have for improving the dealership?" Ralph asked, smiling.

"Yes," Charlie snapped without hesitation, "that son of yours ain't worth a damn."

Ralph thought Charlie was kidding. "That bad, huh?" Ralph replied with a smile.

"Worse than bad, Mr. Ralph. He's hated by everybody on the lot, and he ain't even ever around. Imagine what people would think if he ever showed up for work."

Although Ralph showed surprise and shock, he already knew this. Greg had been irresponsible in his teens. Why would being anointed president of operations change that? Ralph made one adjustment in the company's organizational chart. Did he fire Greg? No, he hired a very experienced general manager at $250,000 a year and promised him an additional $50,000 bonus to accept the title Vice President of Dealership Operations.

Greg's golf handicap is now in the single digits, and last year he won the County High Desert Amateur Motocross trophy. Mechanic Jim makes up Greg's one-man pit crew.

In the presence of the super-rich, most of us act like Ralph's employees. We often subjugate ourselves to someone else's authority and process because we assume they "know best." In doing so, we allow ourselves to fall victim to the Peter Principle, relinquishing our ideas and abilities for the sake of playing by someone else's rules.

## INSTANT CREDIBILITY

A nonprofit theater-arts organization was failing. They needed a quick infusion of cash in order to complete their season of performances and survive to plan and promote the next one. At an emergency board meeting, one of their wealthiest donors spoke up.

In a dreamy voice, she described the grand performances she had attended in her childhood. "I remember walking in through huge, heavy glass doors. The first thing we did was to buy popcorn and drinks at a shiny, gold counter. Then we enjoyed the show. What an event!"

She continued, "If only we offered a real event. People should feel welcomed the minute they walk in the door . . . I know what we're missing! We need to build a beautiful, shiny, golden café and serve drinks and snacks before and after each performance. I'll chair the project and donate $500,000 to get it started."

Just like that, the deal was sealed. The people in the room shifted uneasily in their chairs, looked at one another, and began to offer their congratulations. "Genius!" "We'll double our sales." "This will really set us apart!"

Even though the wealthy donor had no business or fundraising experience, the theater director and board of directors bowed to her dollars and acquiesced to her plan. Within three months, her architect had designed a grand lobby makeover, complete with a handmade Venetian-glass bar. Two contractors, six months, and $1.6 million later, the theater reopened their doors. No one came. The organization folded within the year.

This donor's money bought her instant credibility . . . and ultimately, great embarrassment. We've spoken about the incident several times, and she feels the responsibility and the failure keenly. It's not much fun to go from savior to scapegoat.

## I'D RATHER BE RICH

Wouldn't you like to be rich—to live the lifestyle and be given the authority? Of course you would. You've said so many times: "If I just had money, people would respect me." "I would love to have someone ask my opinion, but I'm not rich so nobody cares what I think." "If I had money, I would feel better about myself." "I'm smart, but I just can't get a break." "Why not me?" We have all had such thoughts at one time or another. I used to think them often, until I realized every time I place the rich on a pedestal, I put myself down.

Don't buy into the fiction. The rich—just like the rest of us—know when our opinion stinks. So do they. We know when we are guessing or when we have diligently constructed our thoughts. So do they. But when we are wrong, our friends, family, or coworkers generally call us on our inaccuracy or indiscretion. When we are challenged, we learn, we grow, we evolve, and eventually we hone solid knowledge and skills.

A super-wealthy person may pontificate about politics, sports, or even fashion just because he can; the rich know we are listening, and they know we believe them based on what they have rather than on what they actually know. They often surround themselves with "yes" men who are paid to tell them what they want to hear. Before long, they secretly stop believing in their own opinions. Then they begin to distrust those who don't care enough to challenge what they say is right. The super-rich end up like the emperor with no clothes—being ignored by the very audience they hope to impress.

Being wealthy does not make you smarter. Admittedly, some individuals have increased their wealth by being demonstrably superior in one field. But my experience is, collectively, the rich yearn for honesty and objectivity. Clients complain they do not want people to compromise their real thoughts and opinions about a subject. They want the truth. They want to be challenged. They want to debate. They want to be right—when they really are.

The next time you are in the presence of someone you are tempted to believe simply because of their wealth, try something. When they finish expressing an opinion you believe is incorrect, say the following: "Interesting . . . but I disagree."

Watch the individual's face. You will see a flicker of shock and disbelief. Pause for a moment, and think carefully about your response. Speak your opinion honestly and boldly. I guarantee the other person will listen intently. Perhaps you'll begin an argument or heated debate. Regardless, you will have earned their trust and respect.

# CHAPTER THIRTEEN

# MYOPIC VISION

The super-rich often develop myopia, focusing much attention on small details rather than looking at the big picture. Their priorities are often skewed; their goals and desires are constantly shifting because there is so much available to them. Yesterday's desire may be passé, replaced today with a new ambition or craving that turns in a totally different direction.

## A NARROW WORLD

Before long, the super-rich can become nearsighted, seeing only what is right in front of them. Their world can become very narrow.

Through this behavior, the rich rope themselves off from much of the world. Life becomes very limited. The super-rich may have plenty of material things, but they don't get to hear the truly honest thoughts and ideas of people of lesser means. They miss out on the chance to learn from successes and failures, from winning and losing, from profit and loss. They wall themselves into an artificial world with a captive audience rather than a life lived in grimy reality and with genuine relationships. They rarely experience the richness and fulfillment of day-to-day existence, because they live on top of the world as opposed to in the world.

There is a property on the beach in California. It is not buildable. Why? Because of a rock—actually, a small mountain. In the middle of this one-acre lot, a rock formation that reaches 80 feet into the air has prevented, until now, a home from being built at sea level or at the top of the rock, which has no access.

Enter the local billionaire, named Layton. He and his third wife look at the property, and she says "It's perfect! A place for the family to relax and enjoy sunsets!" The realtor, true to professional form, replies, "I can see your home now!"

The property was listed for $22.5 million, including beach rights, if you could get to it. There wasn't much haggling as the property owner knew the only offer he had received in three years had to be from a buyer who would pay anything. They settled on a purchase price of $21 million. The seller included a four-year-old $2,000 environmental study that indicated the lot was not buildable. Layton was willing to bet about $21 million it was.

Layton then hired the most renowned architect in the region and went through his vision for the home. Unfettered by financial constraints, the architect amassed a list of details that were fabulous; for example, a swimming pool over the eight-car garage on the main part of the property was to be connected to the home by a bridge entryway. The multilevel home on stilts would include a master bedroom suspended 80 feet above the ocean, with a glass bottom allowing the residents to keep a vigil on the tide (lighted at night with underwater flood lights, of course). The price and time for completion? Who knew? But that was unimportant. The vision moved onward, in increasing detail. The only limit to the design was the owners' imagination.

This is what I characterize as managing expectations from the top down. In other words, if I can dream it, then I can have it. Most people manage their expectations from the bottom up: How much can I afford to achieve something that will be as close as possible to my desires? If it is too expensive, then my expectations will have to decrease.

To visualize what was going on in Layton's world, let me use the design of the wine cellar alone. As a have not, if you were interested in storing wine, you would first entertain the purchase of a U-line Wine Storage model from Costco (price: $300) and put it in your garage. Expectations for wine preservation met. But Layton likes to preserve about 2,500 bottles of vintage wine, so his first requirement was a large room. Next, the room must be cooled to the perfect temperature. But the white wine may be chilled a little more if it is to be served immediately upon selection; hence, there will need to be two independent cooling systems, which requires a sealed divider in the room: a door. The door shouldn't obscure the visual scope of the entire wine collection, so it must slide and be made of glass. But because glass doors transmit temperature, a double-insulated, vacuum-sealed glass door is preferable.

To prevent the bottles from getting dusty, there must be an electronic particle filter connected to the cooling system. Some of the wine bottles are each worth several thousand dollars or more. Those need to be displayed individually, in wood cradles. But what about the type of wood for the whole wine cellar? It could be a typical variety, but there are several African or Brazilian woods that would add a unique ambience to the room with a slight hint of wood smell, like a mild cedar.

What about lighting inside the cellar? Down-lights might be adequate. But adequate is the minimum, and Layton doesn't do minimum. He decided to install a variety of lighting systems that automatically turned on when someone entered the room. As motion detectors sensed someone's movement toward a particular wall of wine, that wall gradually would illuminate from dim to just light enough to read the labels on the bottle. The expensive bottle cradles are separately lit; micro tube lighting is recessed into the wood frame around each bottle that is displayed as you walk into the entrance to the cellar.

For the floor of the cellar, wood, brick, or tile would be the typical options. Layton decided to bid on a historical stone floor from a three-century-old wine cellar in the Loire Valley of France. Besides, he needed to cover only 720 square feet of floor space. Including shipping, the floor (uninstalled) cost only $270 a foot, for a total of $194,000. The floor did offer a "no wax" finish.

Try to keep in mind the purpose of this house for Layton and his wife was to have a barbeque once in a while at a summer beach house. Did I forget to mention this was a vacation home, one of six homes Layton owns in four countries? And remember, this was just the wine cellar, one of eighteen rooms in the residence.

As a result of local coastal authority and environmental objections to Layton's proposed home, it took five years to obtain the building permits, along with almost $1 million in legal fees to fight the battles, each of which required Layton's attention and sometimes attendance at hearings. For the most part he was not upset, as he recognized these were just hurdles he needed to clear in order to reach the finish line. Tell me again where the finish line was?

The actual construction began five years ago and is still not complete. What is ironic is the ritual of the construction workers who have been on the project site the entire time. They have made a tradition of setting up a camp stove on the beach and inviting their entire families down on Friday afternoons to grill Mexican fajitas and tortillas. There is a lot of laughter and frolic until everybody pauses to watch the sunset and see who can watch the entire setting without blinking. Even the little ones join in by holding their eyelids open with their fingers. One of the families performed the wedding of their daughter on that very beach. Many family memories have been created over nearly half a decade. And by the looks of it, there will be many more memories to come.

The community by the sea where my wife and I live is touted as a friendly place where people wave and smile at each other as they walk or drive by. But should you try to plant a tree or, even more egregious, actually build a home, you have just invited all your neighbors to a barbecue at the next homeowner's meeting . . . and you are the meat.

When we designed our home, I specifically instructed our architect to adhere to all restrictions imposed by our community, no matter how small or seemingly insignificant. He made sure the ocean views from the other homes were protected, and we worked diligently to avoid doing anything that might upset my future neighbors.

When my wife and I arrived at the community clubhouse to meet with the architectural review board to hear the comments of our neighbors about our home, every one of our future neighbors was already seated. At first, we thought they might have come to welcome us to the community.

But when I scanned the room, I quickly saw each person had a file folder in hand with a set of notes. Not a good sign. Over the next hour, we felt as though we were being run out of Dodge. They hated everything about our new home, declaring even though we had met all of the architectural guidelines, our request to build should be denied. One of the board members suggested we consider building in a different community. My wife began to cry and left the meeting.

Later, a neighbor explained to me the negative review was a rite of passage, a ritual, a dance of sorts to appease territorial residents who protect their castles as if they were being invaded. After we completed our home, I was actually invited to participate in terrorizing new residents with similar hopes of building a dream home. Instead, I invited the new neighbor over for a drink.

## THOSE WHO "GET IT"

Where do satisfaction and fulfillment come from when achievement is meaningless? What happens when there aren't any needs to meet or provisions to acquire? Many of the rich who have run dry of spiritual capital because they have been exhaustive in fulfilling personal wants choose a cause and become philanthropists. Keep in mind the great majority of people give away only a small fraction of what they have—and in most cases, this giving is not really sacrificial. It doesn't jeopardize the fortune or cause the super-rich to change their lifestyles. But it does provide them a sense of satisfaction and fulfillment, a feeling of doing something for the greater good, a sense of selflessness in a world that reeks of self.

Don't get me wrong; it is amazing to be able to do something special to benefit others. I greatly respect those who give away some of what they've been given for the sake of somebody else. Deep down, we all want to make a difference. We all say to ourselves, "If I had that kind of money, I'd help so and so or support such and such." It's pretty incredible to be able to do some of these things.

But what I am suggesting is the super-wealthy generally don't get the same satisfaction from giving $1 million as you do by rolling up your sleeves and pitching in. It is not as much their loss as your gain. Too often the giving of the super-rich includes attaching their name to the live auction bid of $25,000 for a Hershey's extra-large chocolate bar. It is the private donor you need to respect. But given that you don't know who they are, then respect what they stand for—helping without reward.

At a fund-raiser I once witnessed a request by the MC for anyone who might be willing to donate any amount of money to the charity. After a few raised hands pledging $100 and $500, and a couple at $1,000, a well-known real estate broker, Fred Waters, stood up and challenged, "I will donate $100,000 if someone will agree to match me." What a statement. He challenged the whole gala, called them out to the O.K. Corral for a shoot-out that would determine who was the big fish in the community. The five-hundred attendees sitting at their tables went silent. Completely unnoticed, a distinguished gentleman in a tuxedo left the table, apparently to use the restroom. After several minutes passed with almost no sound, one of the coworkers for the event entered the same door the gentleman had left and approached the microphone. Her eyes were filled with tears of joy; she could hardly talk. She was not experienced in speaking but was so filled with excitement that she stepped in front of the MC and with a soft voice announced to the audience, "We have just received a matching donation of $100,000 from a donor who has insisted on remaining anonymous. This wonderful man has agreed to match Fred Waters' $100,000 donation and pledge an additional $50,000."

As the room roared with applause, I noticed the same smartly dressed gentleman quietly enter via the exit door and re-take his seat. It was an expensive trip to the men's restroom, and he got it right.

## EXPANDING OUR HORIZONS

How can we avoid myopia and experience the full spectrum of humanity? It's so simple. Spend time with people. Engage with that part of humanity that faces down the realities of life every day—the servers, car washers, and gardeners. Talk to your housekeeper, a policeman, a pastor, or a teacher. Go to a picnic with your neighbors, ask for their opinions, and listen. Join a small group from your church that holds meetings in a neighborhood coffee shop. Throw a potluck dinner, and dare to invite people from outside your usual circles.

Alfredo owns an auto detail company and drops by my house to wash my car on Wednesdays. He is as hard a worker as anyone on the planet. He treats everyone—great and small—with genteel respect, as if they were royalty. When he finishes my car, I always praise his work and shake his hand. At first, my gesture seemed awkward for him. Each time I asked how he and his family were doing. He started answering with a canned "Fine." But then I intentionally asked him a second question, "Do you enjoy your family?" The answer was a quick and respectful "Yes." My next question didn't let him off so easy: "What do you and your family like doing best?" He grinned and began to describe his kids' latest and greatest accomplishments.

Alfredo is now my friend. One time I referred his wife to a doctor who helped her deal with the depression she'd been suffering for years. It changed their married life. When I shake his hand now, he tears up. He is so grateful. But don't mistake my acts as benevolence or charity. I truly recognize him as a person. He details cars; I am a lawyer. What gives me the right to separate myself? If I needed help, I have no doubt he would be there the next day. I would do the same for him.

# CHAPTER FOURTEEN

# LEADING *a* DOUBLE LIFE

Ron and Ellen are prominently figured in every local magazine story covering charity or philanthropic events in Los Angeles. Ellen was forty-five, and Ron was nearly sixty. This was the second marriage for both, and they each professed to have found their soul mate. From the outside, they seemed to be living the life all of us were intended to live.

## ON THE OUTSIDE

After nearly seven years of marriage, Ron and Ellen showcased their amiable relationships with their ex-spouses and children. Though neither had primary custody, they traveled regularly on "educational" trips to Europe and Asia as a blended family. Ron and Ellen argued the expense of these trips—although they were only biannual—equalized the time commitment between them and their ex-spouses in regard to the children. In reality, the trips served as a financial payoff that permitted Ron and

Ellen to maintain extensive travel and social calendars through-out the remainder of the year. Unfortunately, this arrangement meant Ron and Ellen missed out on much of their children's growing-up years.

Ron had several homes, including a mansion on the Snake River in Washington. He threw an annual retreat for his buddies, offering a week of fishing and fun complete with professional cooks, incredible food, boats, fishing guides, tackle, accommodations, and a fountain of liquor. If the fishing became slow or tiring, Ron's local country club boasted a stunning golf course with all green fees paid. After four days of rising at dawn and coming back to the house after a successful catch, everyone would sit around the fire pit and share stories until past midnight, only to rise four hours later to repeat the day. In the realm of high society, holding a spot on the annual guest list was like flashing a commissioner's badge to a traffic cop.

Ellen seemed like the perfect wife: tolerant, patient, and uncomplaining. She said she was happy to see her husband and the "boys" having a little fun on the river. The other men thought, "If only our own wives wouldn't hold us hostage to a list of fix-its and honey-do's when we get home." They relished their brief escape.

Some years, Ron arrived late or left early because of the demands of his business. He took it all in stride, making sure his guests would enjoy their time at the "castle" as long as they liked. Looking back, I remember bantering about whether we would want to stay an extra week in paradise or enjoy the prestige and excitement of having our vacation interrupted like

Ron, as we watched his private helicopter land on the grassy riverbank and whisk him to the waiting Learjet at a nearby airport. Most of us decided it would be worth giving up our prized fishing time if we could buzz around to work on flying machines with private pilots.

## ON THE INSIDE

Ellen's grown children from her former marriage were a mess. Her son Adam struggled with drugs; he had spent time in rehab twice and needed to return for a third stint. Her daughter, Stacy, finalized a divorce from one man and moved in with another, the father of her child. Little Casey, age two, spent a lot of time with Grandpa Ron and Grandma Ellen. This "stellar" couple doted on the child, and they were a picture of loving support in the eyes of their family and community. But in reality, Casey wasn't visiting. She was living with Ron and Ellen under the care and rearing of their housekeeper.

Ron kept both of Ellen's children on the company payroll, basically to keep them from pushing shopping carts on the street. Ellen secretly threatened her children every month, telling them this was going to be the last time she would bail them out of credit-card debt. Ellen believed she could ask Ron to support her children only through their jobs with his business. Any extra handouts came from her budget. Ron knew the ins and outs of the situation, but he played the game to maintain a level of pressure, keeping the financial drain in check.

In reality, Ellen's son played Ron like a fiddle. Ron had two girls, and he had always wanted a boy. Although Adam didn't exactly fit the picture of the perfect son, Ron had spent his own childhood begging forgiveness from his parents. By forgiving Adam, he was forgiving himself. The arrangement supplied Ron and Adam with precious additions to their lives: a son and cash, respectively.

## ON THE OTHER SIDE

In the ninth year of his marriage, Ron privately disclosed his affair with Susan, a younger woman in Indianapolis. Ellen didn't know, and he meant to keep it that way. Susan and the two toddlers Ron had fathered with her didn't know about Ellen either. His second family was living a "normal life" in Indiana with no idea daddy's business was more diversified than most.

Matters became even more complicated. Ron was concerned the prenuptial agreement Ellen had negotiated expired after ten years of marriage. In other words, if they remained married for six more months, Ellen would have a clear shot at Ron's exposed financial target. If they were to divorce, he would lose hundreds of thousands of dollars in spousal support. Ron decided to play Texas Hold 'Em with his life, and by doing so he raised the stakes on a hand that couldn't win.

Almost exactly one year later, Ellen found Susan's Indiana driver's license in Ron's sport coat pocket. Two weeks earlier,

Ron had unknowingly slipped it into his pocket while checking in for a flight to Disneyland with Susan and their two kids at the Delta counter in the Indianapolis International Airport. Before confronting Ron, Ellen sent a letter by Federal Express to Susan asking her to call. The conversation that followed brought two women living two thousand miles apart to the brink of conspiracy to commit murder.

The events in the biblical book of Job seem like an improvement over the next five years of Ron's life. The divorce lawyers in Indianapolis and Los Angeles formed a feeding frenzy. There were four sides to this battle—Ron, Ellen, Susan, and Ron's ex-wife, Mary, who seized on the opportunity to leverage a bid for increased support. Ron had to finance the extravagant lifestyles of all four. Imagine buying a fireworks warehouse and then lighting a campfire inside.

After a while, everything for Ron came down to business. I think Ron knew it would eventually. He is smarter than the rest of us, and we always knew it. He paid dearly, no doubt, but his pile of riches seemed infinite. Ellen's final amount of spousal support was the only surprise. She did not get as much as she had hoped. Not long after the litigation began, Ron's lawyers discovered Ellen had maintained an ongoing sexual affair with her personal trainer. Duplicity indeed.

Ron is now married for the fourth time. The annual fishing trips have stopped. Ellen received the river house in the settlement. But Ron still has a five-star life, and the new friends he and his fourth wife, Chefron, have acquired revel in Ron's largesse.

## ALL BETS ARE OFF

Nathan and Marilyn appear happily married and are considered two of the community's great pillars. They heavily support three of the country's most popular charities and are praised in most circles. Nathan is an avid golfer and Marilyn a committed shopper. She is known for being a coupon clipper, unafraid to present the local grocery store with a two-for-one discount coupon for ketchup. Marilyn gets kudos from her friends and social circles for being conservative.

Nathan's favorite golf destination is Las Vegas, Nevada, originally because Nathan was frugal and liked to stay in great rooms at a reasonable price. Over the years, Nathan became a fan of blackjack. A decade ago, he hated losing bets of any size: $1, $2, or $5. As his life came to need a boost, Nathan began to up his bets on the golf course from $2 per hole to $20 per hole. After golf and a shower, Nathan would find himself at the blackjack table. It was a strange feeling for Nathan to win money or even lose money easily. It gave him a rush. After a couple of years of golfing in Vegas once a month, the size of his bets increased. It was no longer about winning or losing for Nathan; it now was about the thrill of his gambling destiny being outside his control.

Nathan was used to controlling everything in his world. Now a dealer would flip an ace and Nathan felt the rush of success. Sitting at a special table for a minimum wager of $2,000 brought gawking crowds. Nathan winked at the onlookers as the dealer scooped up a pile of five $1,000 chips. He knew the women surrounding him were in awe of a guy who could lose $5,000 in one deal of the cards and not even care. In fact, when the crowd grew large Nathan would cover three empty spots on the table with five $1,000 chips each. That's $15,000 in one bet! He could sense the tension as the audience waited for the deal. There was an even greater rush to losing than to winning. To win $15,000 was no big deal, but to be able to sit calmly while those around gasped at a loss was exhilarating.

Periodically Nathan would invite a beautiful woman from the crowd to sit down and play a hand for him at his expense. If she won, he would hand her a $1,000 chip and say, "Honey, treat yourself to a nice dress or a piece of jewelry . . . on me." These women were much younger than Marilyn and hung on his every word. And occasionally the same women would repeatedly keep Nathan company in Las Vegas. Nathan became well known to the casinos in Vegas as he might typically lose in excess of $500,000 in one weekend.

Marilyn, on the other hand, was shopping for clothing—specifically, shoes. Her walk-in closet stored five hundred pairs of shoes. Each rack was filled, and new shoes took the place of older ones. In Marilyn's ten-car garage, she had converted a wall into a shoe rack that held another six hundred pairs. They too were filled. Her primary shopping companions refused to cruise the local malls with her, as Marilyn would head to the shoe department and spend hours trying on and then stacking her purchases. She had only one rule: her minimum price per pair was $500, with a target range of around $1,500 per pair.

Marilyn knew about Nathan's gambling propensities. It was

a convenient excuse to permit her excesses in purchasing shoes. Marilyn did not know about the women who had become regulars at Nathan's blackjack table. Nathan did not know Marilyn was sleeping with her thirty-year-old male trainer.

The super-rich can be experts in the art of presenting perfection. They work hard to display a flawless public persona and a carefree, opulent lifestyle. Husband and wife smile and recite a long list of show-stopping experiences and luxurious purchases. It may seem to be a rosy picture, but often what you see is not what you get. Nine times out of ten, what you see is what the rich want you to see.

The have nots believe the haves don't have problems because of their wealth. Equally naïve is the super-rich person who thinks his money buys immunity from the common troubles of the world. A glossy façade hides a multitude of imperfections. Like mold growing in the dark, the problems multiply out of sight.

As normal conflicts and troubles arise, the rich can choose to conceal the truth about themselves from the outside world, and a secret life emerges outside the specter of public criticism. The public sees a picture-perfect family, scads of friends, and a privileged lifestyle. But like a photograph, this life is two-dimensional. Wealth occupies space. Family life for many of the super-rich is not apportioned as much space as the typical family of have nots. The more numerous the distractions in one's life are, the greater the need to shift and re-shift priorities among them. Most people do not care about your average family. But the family of the super-rich is sometimes considered a show-piece to the community. They want you to know the family flies in a private jet on holiday to Aspen. They prefer you not know the nanny didn't succeed in rearing the children to become responsible adults. Wealthy families often fail to recognize that flaws and imperfections give depth and richness to life.

How quick we are to buy into the hype. We are all guilty of swallowing the bait, foisting ourselves onto the hook at the end of a line that leads to someone who is merely fishing their way through life, creating drama to satisfy their ego, and using the general population as an endless supply of worms. The next time you wish for a five-star life, visualize the food chain. And remember, the chances of being consumed increase the higher you climb.

The super-rich feel pressure. But the pressure to confirm and re-confirm money does in fact cure all ills. We all grow up believing winning the lottery is the blue ribbon event of life's experiences. How often have you felt sorry for a rich person? Even if they experience the normal setbacks of day-to-day life, we are reticent to cut them slack. We become unforgiving because the rich should be able to fix any problem with money. I recently attended a dinner where a guest remarked that a super-rich family had a seventeen-year-old daughter who was struggling with a severe bipolar disorder and was near suicidal. Another guest smiled, "That little bitch drives a new Porsche Cayenne and is heading off to an all-expenses-paid private college. What has she got to be depressed about?" That pressure to maintain appearances sometimes creates behavior that can be obsessive. Obsessions are things nobody likes to admit. The obsessions of the super-rich are just more extravagant.

# CHAPTER FIFTEEN

# SPIRITUALLY CHALLENGED

*Money never made a man happy yet, nor will it. There is nothing in its nature to produce happiness. The more a man has, the more he wants. Instead of its filling a vacuum, it makes one. If it satisfies one want, it doubles and trebles that want another way. That was a true proverb of the wise man, rely upon it: "Better is little with the fear of the Lord, than great treasure, and trouble therewith."*

—*Benjamin Franklin*

It has been suggested there is an inverse relationship between spirituality and the increase of one's wealth. Two factors contribute: the focusing of more time on preserving and increasing wealth, and the distraction of materialism and self-promotion.

Granted, one who becomes wealthy as an atheist will likely stay an atheist. The challenge comes for the spiritual man who becomes super-wealthy. Both might find struggle in not succumbing to the personal decay of probity. The atheist may land in an abyss of dissatisfaction and lack of fulfillment, while the spiritual man might more likely experience a sense of worth-lessness and disappointment.

Both the old and new testaments of the Bible reflect on it.

*Whoever loves money never has enough; whoever loves wealth is never satisfied with his income. This too is mean-ingless. As goods increase, so do the wants of those who con-sume them. And what benefit are they to the owner except to feast his eyes upon them? The sleep of a laborer is sweet, whether he eats little or much, but the abundance of a rich man permits him no sleep.*

*—Ecclesiastes 5:10–12*

Timothy repeats a similar theme:

*People who want to get rich fall into temptation and a trap and into many foolish and harmful desires that plunge men into ruin and destruction. For the love of money is the root of all kinds of evil. Some people, eager for money, have wan-dered from the faith and pierced themselves with many griefs.*

*—1 Timothy 5:9–10*

## TIME SPENDS ONLY ONCE

Your life can be sliced like a pie into three pieces: your personal journey, your family and friends, and your spirituality—said another way: yourself, those around you, and your belief in a greater purpose or being. You have only one life, and the pieces, however proportioned, can be no greater than the whole pie. Balancing between them is very important—and, often, not very easy. Wealth tends to expand the opportunity for exploring one's personal journey. But as we make choices to take on new endeavors, businesses, sports, hobbies, etc., the other pieces of the pie must shrink.

There is only so much time. And wealth takes time. In Ray Kroc's book *Grinding It Out*, he writes, "I believe in God, family, and McDonald's—and in the office, that order is reversed." The choice to dedicate more time to building wealth reduces the time one can spend on family and spirituality. Many have argued super-wealth releases more time because people who have it do not have to worry about providing a roof over their own head. That's easy to say, but it's not true. Wealth is not just about preservation, but distraction. It requires you to consider how to preserve what you have, make more, and choose from the myriad of things you can do with it and how you are going to spend it. It consumes time.

Money has a way of perpetuating its own project. Can you imagine if you stepped up to a slot machine and put in $1 and won $100? Your first thought would be, "That was so easy. Think what I can buy. An electronic accessory I don't really need but would love to have? Take my wife to dinner? Pay off the electric bill? Just carry around five extra $20s in my pocket for a while?" But if you could reasonably expect to win again, the first thing you would do is . . . put in another dollar. And when you won again, you would consider the things you could now buy with $200. The list could expand: "Maybe a new blazer, a purse, a pair of shoes?" If you stayed at the slot machine all day, and every time you pulled you returned more money, you would continue day after day cashing in on your good fortune. Each time the pile increased you would delight in the mental survey of the next level of consumables you could now buy. Eventually, you would get everything you could possibly imagine and want. Then what? When you can't give it away because you are invested in the process of growing it, and you have your private jet, and the largest private ship in the marina, you either get a bigger jet or bigger boat, or you just focus your energy on growing the number of zeros.

While spending a holiday on the beach in Maui, Hawaii, with my family, I noticed a man sitting in his bathing suit outside of his $6 million oceanfront condominium. His wife and preteen children were frolicking in the ocean in front of him. On his legs he held a laptop, and a second, smaller computer sat on the ground in front of him. Two cell phone holsters were mounted on his beach chair, with two spare batteries Velcroed to the chair's arm. This positioned him for beachside command of his own multiple business enterprises. He used to be the president of a well-known Internet provider, which he had retired from in his early fifties. In six hours I never saw him leave the chair or look up at his kids. He was engrossed in phone calls, typing reports, texting, and e-mailing. He repeated this ritual seven days a week. Building and maintaining wealth is expensive. But the cost is paid in minutes, not dollars.

The devil has an easy job with the super-wealthy. He doesn't need to corrupt them. He just needs to convince them to spend more time away from their spiritual being. Self-corruption is our human specialty. Just let a man or woman take the controls long enough and they tend to detour toward materialism and self-indulgence.

## "MIRROR, MIRROR . . ."

Money often anesthetizes self-inspection and self-actualization. Spirituality is about selflessness: deflecting personal credit and self-reward in the pursuit of the betterment of the lives of others. It's about confidently surrendering control and allowing others to participate and contribute to the decision process: being self-sacrificial and nonjudgmental. Sound like your typical billionaire?

The challenge money poses to the spirituality of the super-wealthy is in defining goals. Life goals are usually defined in terms of the value we assign to personal ambitions. These goals are often lofty, maybe even unattainable, but they are based on a desire to be excellent at something or to arrive at a place in our journey that we rate highly. Money tends to define a goal in terms of itself—namely, to accumulate more of it. If you have $10 million, then you set your goals on $50 million. If you have $100 million, you target $500 million. Instead of reflecting on others, the super-rich become captivated by the reflection of their own story. It is hard to be spiritually fed with the gratitude, love, and respect of others when you are hyper-involved in your own journey.

In ancient Greece there was a feared superstition that it was fatal for one to look at his or her own reflection. In Greek mythology, Narcissus, son of Cephissus, angered the gods by rejecting the advances of the nymph Echo and was condemned by Aphrodite to fall in love with his own image. He sat next to a pool of water, admiring his reflection, until he failed to even nourish himself and eventually died. In psychiatry and especially psychoanalysis, the term narcissism denotes an excessive degree of self-esteem or self-involvement, a condition that is usually a form of emotional immaturity.

People of super-wealth are sometimes unknowingly absorbed in admiring the biography of their own life, which is being written and lived by them contemporaneously. Many of them practice sharing aloud among friends and in public on their ongoing favorite topic: their autobiography. When people are consumed with their own story, there is less room for a greater purpose or a supreme being. Super-wealth is not about being bad, it's about being distracted. Like a Ferrari sitting on the showroom floor, it's all imagination and potential power. It's the test drive that leads to ownership, excessive speed, and in the future perhaps a wreck.

We are all a little guilty of this, but for most of us, reality rears its head and reminds us our lives can be extraordinary only for a while. The realization soon arrives that extraordinary lasts only until the alarm rings on Monday morning and the kids need to be fed, the house cleaned, the laundry done, an eight-hour day worked, and meals made. The gem of life for ordinary people is that extraordinary is just around the corner. If only for a fleeting moment, we have hope it will return.

The process of worldly saturation is slow and many times unnoticeable for the haves. Those few of the super-wealthy who are predisposed to spirituality may successfully avoid becoming victims of self-indulgence and the erosion of their own self-worth. Few will deny the journey is unavoidably a struggle and, in the end, less rewarding than they had anticipated. People who applaud the charity of the super-rich in public can become bearers of jealousy and criticism in the shadows. The super-rich can become callous and numb to those around them because managing one's own story tends to isolate them from normal interactions that bear the naked truth about who they are.

One might argue the charity of the super-rich is evidence of their spirituality. Indeed many of the wealthy who build hospitals and give scholarships to deserving students have good intentions and big hearts. Many are full of charity. But many of the super-wealthy just write a check. It is rarely significant to their relative wealth, yet is met with adulation of the masses. The donors believe they are spiritual and charitable because the masses hold them in high esteem for the gift. But what is in the minds of the super-rich givers? They secretly recognize what the audience really wants is their checkbook. Giving away money becomes boring and unsatisfying. The greatest pleasure for the rich in giving away large sums of money is watching the reaction of the have nots, who are completely delighted and overwhelmed at the thought of so much money being gifted away—a year's salary for most people, in exchange for a puppy or a chocolate bar at a live auction.

On one television reality show rich people disguise themselves and secretly enter the world of the "little people" who are responsible for most of the hard work that makes our national charity efforts work. Not the CEO of the Red Cross, who gives speeches at fund-raisers (although this function is incredibly important), but the retired spiritual Mother Teresas who joyfully give their days, weeks, and months doing their best to help others with no expectation of return for themselves. At the end of the show the millionaire sheds his alias and hands a whopping donation (usually between $10,000 and $50,000) to the neighborhood charity. The subliminal message is interesting. It's like putting a coin in the box of the organ grinder and watching the monkey dance. The charity workers who receive the gift start jumping up and down while crying tears of joy! Clapping and singing erupt! The receipt of a gift of $20,000 directly translates in their minds to five-thousand meals for the poor. Their spirits are full. On the other hand, the $20,000 is no big deal for the millionaire. The millionaires usually shed a few tears, because they actually experienced renewal during their disguised adventure passing out bowls and paper plates to the poor in the soup line. But more telling is the awe they feel as they experience the true sincerity they see before them in the giving, selfless, spirited people who are committed to helping others. Afterward the millionaires go back to the hotel, gather their Rolex watches and four-carat diamond rings, jump in the limousine, and roll out of town.

One would think, for the super-rich, the ability to give large sums of money to charity would be like imbibing the ultimate spiritual cocktail. How good it must make them feel to do so much good. However, this is not what typically happens from the perspective of the super-rich. Sure, the rich can and do assist tremendously in the building and funding of many important social causes. But does it give them a high? Not for long. In fact, you might feel the same high when you give a $5 tip to a librarian for helping you find a book. Only she will never forget you. "Why," you ask, "doesn't it thrill the rich to give away large sums of money?" Primarily because many times they are giving it to an institution and they don't get to directly feel the benefit they are conferring. Unquestionably, they understand the importance, and they see the results somewhere down the road, but the gratification is passing.

And then there is the other issue: the professional fundraiser. There is an entire industry of very talented salesmen who are experts at hunting down and harvesting the wealthy population for their cause. Few large fund-raising efforts are executed without such a firm in place, and once they paint their high-net-worth targets, they are like cruise missiles. They are professional relationship managers and perform like professional hunters on an African safari. It is all business, and the super-rich know it well.

One of my clients calls me each year. His family created a foundation with approximately $100 million being held in the foundation—a noble cause. The foundation was initially created because giving money to your own foundation allows a tax deduction on your income. The board of directors is the family. Once the money is deposited in a nonprofit corporation, government regulations require the foundation give away five percent per year. The government wants you to donate money you already agreed to give away. In fact, you could give all of the money at one time to one charity. But the family didn't get rich by giving money away. Handing someone a check for nothing in return is hard for them. It made sense as a tax deduction, but the charitable intent ended there. The only money that leaves their foundation is the federally required 5 percent. Every year I get a call from the dad because it is both unexciting and annoying to give away $5 million a year, and they ask for suggestions on whom to give it to. Why not make the choice themselves? They are fearful if they choose a charity, the charity will receive the gift this year . . . and return with its fund-raising professional next year to ask for more.

Many of the super-wealthy are fortunate enough to reach a place in the latter part of their lives when they clearly see their earthly fortune has been a serious distraction. Moreover, they know they have spent precious time accumulating wealth they could not spend in ten lifetimes, at the expense of time and their own personal contentment, which they ignored while they busily increased their empire. Ironically, if they find their spiritual center again, they return to doing the same things they loved to do before they became super-wealthy. And when money and material things no longer occupy both their thoughts and words, they invariable confess, "Life in its simplest form is the only meaningful way to live." There is a lesson there for us all.

# PART FOUR

## I'D RATHER NOT BE RICH

## CHAPTER SIXTEEN

# THE MYTH *of* MIDAS

King Midas loved gold more than anything in the world. He was granted one wish: that everything he touched would turn to gold. Midas delighted in his newfound fortune as he turned everything in his path to gold. Yet he still wanted more—until one day he touched his beloved daughter, who turned into a statue. Midas came to loathe what he at first thought was the greatest of gifts.

In moments of uncertainty, the life of the average person can shine like precious metal. The have nots are versed in the basic necessities of life: food, shelter, companionship, family, and friends. Each day they wake to earn enough to cover the cost of these essentials. Often the average family makes necessary tradeoffs to survive, "If we spend less on shelter, we'll have extra for enjoying outings together." But spending more on shelter may result in too little left for food or other needs. Life requires constant balancing. Most people find a sense of security and peace when the essentials are covered . . . a sense the super-rich may not appreciate.

What have we learned about wealth and its effect on the

long-term treasures a simple life affords? Is there a fix for the wealthy who find themselves described in one or more of these chapters? Is there a lesson for the have nots?

## FLYING AT 30,000 FEET

Let's look at the bigger picture—call it "flying at 30,000 feet." Most large things on the ground look quite small from five miles up. Identifying the "big picture" essentials of your life always involves asking the question, "How is this thing I am considering going to affect every other thing in my life?" At a minimum, every new direction is going to take time. How much time? Is it worth the offset of less time with the family? Is it going to affect your health? What about friendships, your hobbies, your pastimes, your sleep? Ask yourself what are the most important things you want to accomplish in your life during the short time you are on the planet? Does this new direction take you closer to that goal? Where do you want to end up in five years? Ten years? Twenty years? When you are seventy? Are you married? How well do you like your wife? Does she require more time?

Create a list of the essential elements of your universe. Anyone who takes off in a direction of achieving monetary success without creating the simplest list of the action items in their own life is destined to aimlessly let life push them around. There are strong currents everywhere. It is important to set a horizon if you want to know where you stand in relation to your ambitions. Being unidirectional and targeting only money and ignoring other facets of your plan is a recipe for burnout.

## FOCUS AND REFOCUS YOUR GOALS CONTINUOUSLY

The goals you set in college are not necessarily your goals once you are out of college and married with kids. And once you start in business, the pull on your time will change the landscape once again. Continuously sit down with people who are close to you and write down bullet points of what is currently on your plate, and how those things assist or interfere with your life plan. To ignore them and just see where your career takes you is asking for trouble.

The super-rich are no different. Once the money starts to increase, the question ought to be, "What will this money allow me to do that I wouldn't have time to do without it?" If that question can't be answered, then you are on the road to making the means of making money your end. If you ever believe accumulating wealth is the finale, and not just a means to do other things, you should write down this statement: "By the time I get enough money to do all the things I want to do with my life, I will not remember what it is I wanted to do in the first place."

Life is what happens in the spaces in between. Have an initial set of goals, change it regularly, and give yourself a grade for the last period since you revised the list the last time. If you deserve a D for poor effort in structuring a life, admit it, and then do something about it.

## TIME IS A GREAT MARINADE

We are all guilty of requiring instant gratification. For the have nots, reality sometimes slows this process. If you want it but can't afford it, you have to wait. But for the super-rich, if you can think it, you can have it. The distance between wanting and having is narrow. With little thought process the wealthy change directions, and (poof!) new homes, new cars, new boats, and extravagant trips—and sometimes new family, new wife, new life.

Before we can meaningfully survey our course and goals, there must be a pause. Consider lining up the size of a purchase or new endeavor. Perhaps the "size" should include both the money and the time it will take. It may not be expensive to start running marathons, but consider the time it will take to train. It is almost a full-time job. Large purchases should require a longer pause. What if before you bought a new car, you waited six months? What effect would that have? Not much. But in denying yourself instant gratification, you will gain an appreciation for what you are looking to acquire. For the super-rich, put a year between the purchases of a second and third home.

Chuck is one of the country's mega-wealthy. He has a son and a daughter. His home is probably worth $30 million, and his getaway house in Aspen cost no less than $8 million. While visiting his daughter, who resided in Rome during a college exchange program, Chuck and his wife fell in love with Italy and, before they left, purchased a home outside of Rome. The following year, they were visiting their son, who was studying in

France, and found the Loire Valley serene. They had the means to easily purchase a piece of that countryside, and before they left the week-long vacation, they bought a chateau in the village of Chinon. Chuck hired contractors in both locations to renovate the properties to his standards. The properties, two years later, are fabulous, authentic, richly appointed . . . and empty. Next time Chuck might consider letting a little time pass, perhaps a year, before acquiring another vacation home.

There are few instant decisions that turn out better because of microwave-speed decision making. Let the idea steep for a while. Make yourself identify how this might affect you or your family, both positively and negatively. Then when you decide to move on it, do it decisively and with conviction. The mere act of waiting will change your approach.

## BALANCE, BALANCE, BALANCE

There are three legs on the table that is your life: you, your family and friends, and your spirituality. Allow one leg to become shorter and the table will not be level and anything you set on it will spill. Don't become entrenched in the "personal" side of your life. Early in a career a young father works until late at night. On Christmas Eve, the bicycle and dollhouse need to be assembled. Crunch time! You just do it! It will be a story you will tell your entire life. Try to see its value from thirty-thousand feet. If you stay at the office until late that one night, what does that do for your career? Not much.

Ask those around you what they think of your skill in balancing the elements of your life. Insist on honesty. We all know people who have mastered this extraordinary balancing act. Don't be afraid. Ask one of them how they do it. You will discover it is not easy. It takes time.

## WHO WILL SAVE THE CHILDREN?

The unintended casualties of the super-rich can be their children. And it is not the child's fault. Like a child born to a drug-addicted mother, the struggle is inherent. There is one simple rule super-rich parents need to recognize in guiding their children: "For everything you give them, you are taking something away."

Find what you are taking away. When you buy them a new car, realize you take away experiencing the effort it takes to earn enough money to buy a car, new or used . . . balancing the value of a new versus a used car . . . the process of discovering how to earn money . . . the development of skills it takes to interact with a boss and coworkers on the job . . . and the decision making required to prioritize saving money for a car rather than buying nonessentials. At least ten life lessons are taken away from teenagers whose parents purchase them a new car.

Can you imagine the lessons lost when a youth is given a job at the family company or inherits millions of dollars? The greatest misconception people have about wealth is believing it is a good thing to leave large sums of money to their children. Most estate planning is done under the design of top estate-planning lawyers who have one directive: pass along as much wealth to the next generation as possible, minimizing the estate tax. Few of these bright lawyers have seen the destruction this wealth creates in the downstream generations. Even small estates—say, a family home worth $400,000—can create a war between siblings, who may find themselves in court destroying all family relationships permanently. It takes only a couple of hundred thousand dollars, given without forethought, to derail one of your children in the future. Think it through carefully and discuss the various possibilities.

One of U.S. history's richest men, Andrew Carnegie, wrote an essay in 1889 entitled "The Gospel of Wealth," in which he argued that simply passing on wealth to children not qualified to maintain and manage it was very dangerous. Before his death in 1919, Carnegie gave away over $350 million to charity—his entire estate!

## THE GIFT OF CONTENTMENT

Do you still want to be super-rich? Be sure to count the cost.

Be content, not because you made it to be super-rich, but because you didn't. Not because you can afford anything you want, but because you can't. Not because the children you and your spouse raised unexpectedly derailed because of money, but because they didn't.

There is great peace and contentment in the possession of a

home, owned or rented, the accomplishments that are a part of your work, the pleasure of a simple hobby, and the privilege of relationships with family and friends. Find comfort in the fact that you probably sleep better on the $6 pillow you bought at Walmart than the super-rich do on their $500 hand-stitched feather pillows. Living below the world's radar allows you freedom to explore, to make mistakes unnoticed, to take yourself less seriously, and to create your own life story without uninvited social editors.

Understanding the reality of wealth will provide an honest, comparative reflection of your condition. You may discover your world is actually richer than that of the super-rich—in relationships, satisfaction, experiences, and fulfillment. Once you see inside their daily troubles, you might think of your place in life as a safe and welcoming refuge.

When you compare your life to theirs, instead of jealousy feel gratitude that you have less than they do, that you are able to escape their inherent struggles and the judgmental eyes of the world, making your life their reality show. Living as a have not can have great advantages in being able to experience "the simple life" without having to spend a lifetime trying to find it. Remind yourself of this simple but profound truth:

The richest person is not who has the most . . . but the one who needs the least.

## WE WOULD LIKE TO HEAR FROM YOU

I am interested in learning your personal stories about the difficulties wealth can bring to friends and family. Please visit and share at my website www.fablesoffortune.com. I will contact you regarding possibly publishing your story.